STRANGER THAN FICTION

MYSTERY

Other titles in the Stranger Than Fiction series

Murder
Detection

STRANGER THAN FICTION
MYSTERY

LEO GREX

RR

Ravette Limited

First published in the UK by Robert Hale Limited

This edition published by
Ravette Limited

Printed and bound in Great Britain
for Ravette Limited
12 Star Road, Partridge Green,
Horsham, Sussex RH13 8RA
by William Clowes Limited
Beccles and London

Contents

Introduction

In general true crime mysteries may be divided into two main categories. Those that remain unsolved and those that have been solved. However, in some cases the latter often provides material for contention and not infrequently some of this can be subdivided into certainties and unlikely possibles.

Granted that, the variants can grow with each additional fact or fallacy.

Be that as it may, there is invariably an element of mystery in the structure of the cases included in the present collection, which has been contrived to afford an overall variety in the presentation of each. If upon occasion the essential mystery, whether solved or unsolved, encroaches upon the fantastic this is merely in the nature of mysteries of all kinds, particularly in real life, where the exceptional is more often than not proved to be the everyday, as countless detectives have demonstrated repeatedly.

Especially is this the case in mysteries that remain unsolved. For in certain of these unsolved cases lack of solution is not to be confused with lack of result. But in that respect the reader must consider himself or herself in the position of a member of a jury searching for a final verdict.

Such a search is always a challenge.

It is also a good way to make an occasional surprising and personal discovery if one is interested in narrative detection.

Otherwise they are simply good stories from real life.

Once more there are eleven very different cases ranging world-wide and covering many changing years in time. All have their own particular and individual quality of appeal when focusing on a mystery and no two are similar in overall reader interest.

Yet all are fascinating as compulsive true-life dramas.

L.G.

1

ENGLAND

The Killer who was too Helpful

There was a calculating look on the face of the soldier who was careful not to be observed. He had camouflaged himself with a screen of greenery as he watched the camp, and was particularly cautious about avoiding cigarette ends and burned-down match-sticks. Every so often his interest returned to the one-room Nissen-style hut with its wooden slats to the walls, and his eyes narrowed speculatively. At the moment the hut was not occupied, a fact which made it of more than passing interest.

The soldier, who wore the single chevron of a lance-jack, lay on his stomach and considered the hut, for on certain days of each week that hut became a bank. It stood in an isolated place on the outskirts of Bordon Camp. More, as the soldier saw with growing interest, it was almost concealed by a tall privet hedge in need of clipping. On one side was a road, but this did not approach closer than thirty yards away and was shielded by the green hedge. While on the other three sides of the hut there was an assortment of trees, mostly pine of varying heights, which not only enclosed the hut, but provided seclusion from the other properties in the neighbourhood.

The corporal nodded his satisfaction. He had gone over the details both in his mind's eye and with a visual check. But he had to make sure he didn't dawdle. In, out, and away. That was his plan. The only risk he ran was being seen, and he reduced the possibilities of being taken by surprise. He considered he had been clever, and was inclined to pat himself on the back for arranging things as he had.

He squirmed around to make himself more comfortable, lifting himself to his knees and pushing a finger under his First World War tunic to loosen it. Slowly he climbed to his feet, stared between the trees, and after taking a last quick look around him sauntered away, manner very casual and unhurried. He returned to the camp by a roundabout route, whistling between his teeth.

But there was nothing jaunty in the whistle. It was reedy and anxious-sounding. The soldier was young, still in his teens.

His examination of the hut was only one of several he made. Each time he glanced anxiously at the sky. April clouds were scudding across it and there was the threat of a quick downpour. He came to the decision that the afternoon would be his best time, early.

'In, out, and away,' he repeated to himself under his breath. It was like a litany or chant.

He merged with the stream of men from the famous camp.

Some time later William Edward Hall, the bank manager, was making his usual preparation for what he knew was to be his busiest day of the week. The next would be pay-day for some six thousand troops who were stationed at the camp, and William Edward Hall had many ledger entries to make in preparation for paying the soldiers.

He settled down to concentrate on his rows of figures and their trim entries, for the ledgers entailed a considerable amount of work, which he preferred to do without interruption. It was a morning when he did not expect callers, and in any case it was unlikely that he would receive a visit during the lunch hour. He had closed the bank door and was steadily going through his figures and entries for checking when he heard someone knocking.

Surprised, he glanced at the clock. The time was just after two.

'Come in,' he called, and unlocked the door.

There was a pause, as though the newcomer was taking a last look round, and then Hall gasped. A lithe figure bounded in and swung at the bank manager who was in no position to cover his unprotected head.

'No—no—' was all he had time to cry aloud, and then he was beaten senseless.

He sprawled among the piles of copper and silver coins and then his hand slid down. There was blood on his head.

No one else came into the hut that was a bank, and when a Mr Brooker looked for his friend Hall to join him at the bus stop it was almost five past three. Hall was never known to be late, but when the bus came into sight there was no sign of the bank manager.

Mr Brooker ran into the road to see if he could hurry his friend, but for once Hall had failed to appear. The other caught his bus and swung aboard, and the bank manager still had not appeared at the end of the road leading to the bank. Brooker leaned across to the driver.

'Give my friend a couple of minutes,' he called. 'He's always on time. I'll hurry him up, driver.'

The bus driver nodded, stared at the face of his watch, and said, 'Two minutes then, or I'll be running late.'

The three-five bus for Farnham remained with engine ticking over while Brooker ran down the side-road towards the hut. But on that April day in 1924 the bus went on without its two regular passengers.

Brooker found the door of the wooden bank locked. He rattled the door, but couldn't open it. That was when he observed a small round hole in a window pane. He gazed at it, certain that it was a bullet hole. He dashed round to the back, and there saw the body of his friend Hall stretched out on the floor behind the counter.

He was dead, as Brooker saw, for there was a hole in his forehead, and the wound had bled profusely.

Like a man in a daze, he heard the bus pulling away. He stared down at his dead friend and glanced away, shivering. For the first time in his life he felt genuinely solitary. He pulled himself together and turned away. He started to run, intent on raising the alarm.

It was not long before Superintendent William Jones was listening to the report of a shooting in his district. He learned that the shot man was dead. There seemed no doubt that the shooting had been deliberate, and as suicide could be ruled out that made it murder. Jones had no liking for the problems this called to mind.

He questioned Brooker about his friendship with Hall; his questions were promptly answered. William Edward Hall was very much a home-lover. He had a wife of whom he was very fond and their four-year-old child was doted on. Hall himself was a pleasant man, ready to give a helping hand to anyone who asked his help. Punctuality was a creed with him.

'You could set your watch by Bill,' said one friend to whom Jones had spoken.

Yet the bank manager died in his back room of the hut when three bullets were fired, but although Jones questioned everyone closely in the neighbourhood of the Army camp no one seemed to have heard the shots. Jones seemed puzzled by this.

'Damn it,' he exclaimed irritably to a colleague, 'someone must have heard the shooting besides the murderer.'

One of the bullets had smashed into the dead man's shoulder, while another had torn through his neck, ripping a nasty hole in the flesh and emerging from the forehead not far above the left eye. The third had missed its close target of warm flesh. This was the one that drilled through the window pane, making the hole Brooker had observed.

However, motive was easy to determine. Hall had been shot and robbed, and the killer had been in a hurry, but what the superintendent held in reserve was the single question—was the killer a soldier?

If he had been, had Hall recognized him among the thousands in the camp. It was just barely possible, for it seemed likely that the murderer had approached close to his victim before levelling his weapon and squeezing the trigger.

An intensive hunt was made for anyone who could provide a clue, but the quest seemed hopeless from the start. At least, that was how Jones saw it. The murderer had not discarded his weapon, and he had chosen his time during the lunch hour with care to avoid being seen approaching or emerging from the hut. Furthermore, he had chosen a time when the Army pay packets were being made up.

The missing money was checked against the bank manager's books. These revealed that the sum of £698 was missing from the account, made up in single pound notes. Also the thief had vanished with five hundred new ten-shilling notes, while some £110 in other notes was missing, as well as £66 in silver and other coins.

In all, the thief had made a quick haul of a thousand pounds. Presumably he had first murdered the luckless Hall, and then gathered up the loot, which had not taken long, for most of the cash had been packaged for paying out.

The superintendent went over the problem and was convinced that the thief and killer was a soldier who had taken a desperate chance and had got away with it. It also seemed most likely that Hall had let in his murderer. For one thing, the bank manager had been clearly able to perceive anyone approaching. He had a blank window space. Moreover, he had pinned a notice on the outside of the door explaining the times of admission, and the customary practice was to keep this door locked.

But anyone known to the bank manager might very well be admitted.

On the face of it this seemed to be how the killer had gained entry to the bank. It seemed clear that from the work he had been engaged on Hall had not expected an interruption in his figuring. Also, the large leather bag of cash and coins had been dumped and left open on the table under the window, and it was reasonable to suppose that someone had drawn Hall's attention by tapping on the window.

As Jones saw it, the bank manager had most likely walked round the counter in order to answer the locked door, turned the key, and continued away from the person who had attracted his notice, possibly following him into the office where the money was spread. Obviously it had been carefully planned and the manager had been taken completely by surprise. Certainly it was too late for him to prevent the thief stealing the spread of cash. The shots had come in rapid succession.

The bullets had been fired very close to the manager's bared head. There were powder grains in the scorched and shrivelled lips of the wound, which meant that the weapon had been fired at point-blank range.

Then the killer had been in a hurry to collect the money arrayed in anticipation of the Army pay-out. There was a dried pen Hall had put down when he had been interrupted and had unlocked the door to admit his visitor. But there was a dearth of fingerprints, which probably meant that the killer had removed all traces of the gun's handling. He had thrown bundles of Treasury notes into the leather bag together with the bagged silver and had left his victim with blood still oozing from his head wound. Yet one thing had been overlooked by the murderer in his haste.

In a drawer of the desk Jones found the dead manager's loaded revolver. It had been placed on top of the other articles in the drawer and within easy reach of Hall's right hand. Seemingly he had been given no opportunity to get his fingers to it and the murderer was not even aware that the gun was there. The only fingerprints on it were Hall's.

One of the first things Jones did was to instruct a roll-call. Some six thousand men replied to their names. Each man replied. There were no absentees. But Jones couldn't overlook a chance. In consultation with senior officers he now ordered a kit inspection. There was muttering and grumbling in the ranks at this, for the men's equipment had been examined only a day or so before.

The fresh kit inspection drew blank. The NCOs reported no missing kit or weapons. Superintendent Jones was a man who had come for the time being to the end of a short tether. He had to re-examine the obvious. In the same way he had to take a fresh conspectus of local opinion and the various impressions he had received.

For instance, there was the matter of the two statements that had loaned weight to his considerations.

One was made by a signaller, James Haffenden of the 69th Battery of the Royal Field Artillery. He claimed to have called at the bank as near as he could put it at one-fifty that afternoon and had spoken to the manager, who had inquired whether there was likely to be a big pay parade the following day. The signaller had promised to let him know. Later, when Haffenden returned to the bank at about two-fifteen, he was surprised to find the door locked.

'I read the notice pinned to the door,' he told Jones. 'The only thing I could think was that Mr Hall had gone home. I glanced at the window, but the place seemed deserted. I'm afraid I didn't examine the window closely.'

If he had, and gone round the other side to the rear, he might have seen the bullet hole and the manager stretched in death. In that case the alarm would have been raised an hour earlier, when Brooker came looking for his friend.

The other statement considered by the superintendent had been made by Lance-Corporal Jack Goldenberg of the East Lancashire Regiment. He also stated that he had seen the bank manager not long before Hall was murdered. He told Jones that it was about a quarter to two when he entered the bank and had cashed a cheque.

'It was for ten shillings,' he explained to the superintendent, who gathered the impression that the corporal was a loquacious type. He was certainly youthful, and probably liked listening to the sound of his own voice.

'You're sure about the time?' he questioned the man.

'As near as I can be, sir,' said Goldenberg rather smugly. 'But there was something else I saw. I don't know if it's important.'

'Anything's important,' Jones reminded him.

'Well, there was this car that had been parked close by. There were a couple of men in it. Civilians. Can't say I noticed them especially, but now I come to think about it they did seem to be—well, loitering as you might say. You know, sir, hanging about as though they were waiting for something.'

The corporal spoke hopefully. But Jones, a man who was used to receiving quick impressions of a person, considered the soldier was a little too glib, and wasn't impressed by his apparent eagerness to please.

'I couldn't say just how,' he said later, 'but that was certainly the impression he made on me—glib.'

However, with these two statements the time of the crime seemed to be narrowed down to within a quarter of an hour, and the superintendent felt encouraged as the work of searching for possible new clues went ahead by the police. The most important was the reported car with two strangers observed by the corporal. They could have been watching the bank. However, a full inquiry failed to produce anything further about the loitering couple.

No one else had seen them. They were not soldiers. Or at least they had not been in uniform. Goldenberg had not taken particular notice of their faces. He thought one might have had a moustache, but when pressed by Jones he couldn't be certain.

The superintendent had asked, 'Can you describe any single detail of either of them, Corporal?'

He sounded rather testy, and his attitude didn't improve by the reply he received.

'That's the trouble, Superintendent,' said Goldenberg with a rueful grin as he rubbed the corner of his mouth. 'I wasn't really taking much notice of them. Not specially, I mean. Well, why should I? I was in a hurry to get back to camp with the cheque I'd cashed. But someone else might have seen them.'

No one had.

'I have to say it,' said Jones to one of his officers with whom he was discussing the loiterers, 'but Goldenberg seems to have imagined the damned car and the two men. They could have been a mirage.'

'You mean like some figment of his imagination,' said the other dryly.

Jones looked rather grim.

'Best put it this way.' He sniffed. 'The man could have been plain lying, trying to create suspicion for effect. It wouldn't be the first time it's happened, and God knows I don't suppose it'll be the last."

But he put a reserve query against the corporal's name.

Two days later there was a development. A number of stolen notes turned up and were found to be circulating in the camp. The first report was made by a gunner named Tweed of the Royal Field Artillery. An official list of the stolen notes had been issued to personnel, and when Tweed was checking his copy of the list with the notes he had during the following weekend, his sharp eyes noticed that one of the numbers on the list corresponded to the number on a ten-shilling note he had. He went at once to the superintendent.

'Yes, this is one of them,' said Jones. 'Can you tell me where you might have got it?'

'As a matter of fact I think I can,' Tweed explained. 'It was handed to me with some loose change. I remember it because I'd just paid my entrance to a canteen dance. So I'm pretty sure how it came to be exchanged.'

Another of the ten-shilling notes turned up in the possession of a local newsagent, whose shop was patronized by members of the Forces. Jones checked as far as he was able, but then other notes began to circulate in different localities, some of them in the Aldershot district. The camp was swiftly agog with stories of the missing notes being passed, and one of the men who had a keen interest in their passing was Lance-Corporal Goldenberg, who appeared to think that more of the notes might turn up. He discussed the possibility with some of his pals.

'Stands to reason,' he argued, 'that whoever grabbed them isn't going to sit on them, like a clutch of eggs. You can bet on that.'

He sounded confident that his opinion was the right one. Later he discussed the bank-notes with others of his friends and waxed eloquent about his views. He enlarged them to add, 'I'll tell you something else,' and winked knowingly. 'I've got a hunch my evidence will be found to be very important when it comes,' he ended mysteriously.

'How do you mean, Goldie?' asked one of his pals, frowning. 'You been holding back about those two characters you said you saw loitering by a car?'

'No, I don't,' snapped Goldenberg. 'This has nothing to do with them. But I'll tell you something you can remember later. It'll be through me that Mr Hall will be avenged.'

Then he managed another mysterious smile and nodded at his listeners. But he could not be drawn as to the implied meaning of his own words or what they might portend. However, one thing was fairly obvious. The corporal was thoroughly enjoying the sense of baffling mystery he had created.

On another occasion Goldenberg's talkativeness got him into a heated argument about the mysterious couple of so-called loiterers he had seen and the possible make of their car. While the argument continued he consumed five cigarettes quickly, crushing them out one after the other and taking only a few puffs from each. The longer the argument continued the more agitated he seemed to become, and some of his listeners slyly encouraged him with further questions that seemed to increase his agitation. In strenuous rebuttal, he embellished his account with additional details about the two men and their vehicle.

When he stamped out angrily the grins became wider.

'Goldie always was a romancer,' was about the kindest comment any of them made. The bluntest was, 'The silly sod's been caught out in one of his own lies.'

The general opinion was that he would do well to shut up and stop making a bloody fool of himself. But one man who had listened to the back-chat was a certain sergeant-major named Elliott. His private impression was that Goldenberg had been acting strangely, and without saying anything to the lance-corporal he decided to watch the other, especially as the police investigation had come up with nothing except the reported notes. He took to watching Goldenberg while taking care not to be observed himself. He saw that several times Goldenberg appeared to be on the point of approaching a hut where some disused Army equipment had been left, but when he heard someone coming he walked away in a different direction.

What made the sergeant more curious was the fact that this particular hut had been kept locked.

It was about a week after the murder of the bank manager that Elliott, still keeping Goldenberg under secret observation, saw him return, thinking he was unobserved, to the locked hut. After ensuring that no one saw him when he looked around, he nimbly climbed through an open window. At that moment some soldiers came by, one of them whistling. Elliott had to withdraw. The whistler went on with his tune while a couple of his pals talked. By the time the sergeant had concealed himself in a less noticeable place the man he had been observing had vanished with the others. However, at a suitable moment Sergeant-Major Elliott, a man whose sense of mystery had been challenged, produced a key to the locked hut which he had procured, and again taking care not to be seen he quickly turned the key, opened the door, and stepped inside.

Closing the door, he looked around the littered interior of the hut and crossed to the opened window by which Goldenberg, a much smaller man, had entered. Almost at once he saw the marks made by the boot scrapings, where someone had stood on the inside of the sill. There were boot scratches on the white paint where a climber had scrambled up to reach a beam, which was some ten feet or so above the ground.

Elliott was both puzzled and intrigued.

He himself scrambled up to reach a position where he could fit the feet marks to the toes of his own boots. He found that while in this position he had to lean forward to clutch the beam with one hand. However, he was then able to grope with the other, the left. In this groping position he felt something bulky, and withdrew a brown-paper parcel, which he brought into the light and opened.

Inside was a wrapped-up bundle of Treasury notes. Riffling the notes to get a quick idea of their value, he found he was grasping about five hundred pounds.

Elliott climbed down with the parcel of notes and hurried back to put through a call to the camp. He told Superintendent Jones of his find, and within a short time Goldenberg had been arrested and a fresh search made of the hut with the equipment. Police with a reinforcement of Army personnel began a hunt with the aid of torches over a wider area. This went on for some hours into the night. When it was over they had recovered another bundle of hidden notes, smaller than the one Elliott had discovered. It had been screened by leaves and bushes, and apparently was another cache of money Goldenberg had been changing by degrees.

The camp searchers also located a bag containing a quantity of silver coins hidden under some dry straw in an empty room that had recently been used for a court martial. They also came upon a Webley Service revolver, which had been buried in Bordon Wood. The freshly-turned earth was a give away.

Jones was particularly excited by the Webley find. He knew he had found the murder weapon.

Ballistics experts checked that the weapon was indeed the gun that had shot Hall, and when he was confronted by the evidence of his guilt the lance-corporal was only too ready to talk and give his glib tongue free rein. He said he had often gone to the bank, and passed the time of day with Mr Hall, who had always had a pleasant word for the soldiers. It was the sight of the money lying around on pay-day that gave Goldenberg the idea that he could get away with the murder and not be discovered. But there is the possibility that, had it not been for Sergeant-Major Elliott's perception and attention to what he was overhearing, a mysterious murder would have remained a mystery.

At least until a braggart opened his mouth.

After talking to Jones the arrested man said he was prepared to make a formal statement. Written in longhand, this statement said:

'I knew Friday was a silly day to pick on because so many officers would be there. I then decided the next best day would be Monday, but the Monday before it happened was awkward, so I left it day after day, and each day was awkward,' said Goldenberg with an appearance of open frankness that was little short of nauseating.

He even smiled confidently though Jones and the other police officers listened to the words with grave faces. Murder was not something that brought a smile to their faces. Goldenberg's own smile slipped in the face of the continuing grave assembly. He continued more hesitantly:

'On that Thursday I went into the bank about twelve-thirty p.m. and made a passbook payment. I just looked round and went out, deciding to come back again.'

Clearly he was, in the words of the old-time movies, casing the joint. But then his hitherto timid resolve reached the sticking point, or possibly his hands were itching to reach the tempting rolls of notes and piles of silver. But he couldn't remain away for long, but felt drawn irresistibly towards the money.

'I came back,' he went on, 'about twenty to two, and said, "Mr Hall, can you give me an exchange form?" He gave me one, and I went out.'

Seemingly he was still unable to bring himself to shoot the bank manager, but had to force himself to go ahead with the planned shooting. So after a short while he returned. He found the coast still clear, once more glanced about him to make sure he was not observed, and came back. Hall must have been surprised at his reappearance.

'I came back about five minutes afterwards,' went on Goldenberg, 'tapping at the window. The door was shut each time. I just stepped behind the counter and told him to put his hands up. He did not do so, but dived for the drawers beneath the counter, and before I knew it the shot went off.'

Goldenberg had finally reached his fatal sticking point.

'In a flash I realized what I had done, and then, before I realized it, I pressed the trigger again and he fell. I do not know whether the first shot hit him. It seemed as though a red cloud was in front of me, and not for a couple of minutes did I realize what had happened.'

However, standing there with the Webley in his hand and staring down at the fallen Hall, he soon understood what he had to do if he was to get clear away with his crime. He said:

'I took the keys out of his pocket and ran round the counter, which was open, and shut and locked the door. Then I went round the counter and just stood looking. Then I heard a rattle of the door handle. I just ducked down and the person or persons went away. I then opened the drawer, took out all the money and put it in my haversack. I opened the window, went out, and shut the window after me. I went across in front of Colonel Morley's house and came out through the main entrance, and then walked down to the barracks. I went straight into the orderly room and had the cheek to put the money down on to the floor by my chair and set to work.'

By the time he had told his story Goldenberg was smiling confidently again, but the expressions of the men watching him remained blank. Outside the Press were clamouring for the statement, but they had to wait some time till it was signed and dated and the regular procedure followed, for Superintendent Jones was a cautious man who was determined to avoid any legal slip-up.

After the statement had been given to the Press the man now languishing in Winchester Prison had time to reconsider the implications of what he had signed. He now claimed that the killer was a mysterious gunman named Meredith whom he had met on a visit to London. To this unknown Meredith he had described the hut and its surroundings, and his chances of getting away with the shooting.

But it was a thin and threadbare attempt to achieve credibility by a discredited loser, and certainly the jury who heard his second version of the story did not believe him. For them a murder mystery had been solved. They took only a short time to bring in their expected verdict of guilty, and the judge duly pronounced the grim death sentence.

The defence instituted an appeal and a plea of insanity was made on behalf of the prisoner, but the judges who heard the appeal decided that they found no grounds upon which they could interfere with the sentence.

When his last hope of a reprieve vanished Goldenberg sat calmly in his cell like someone in a trance. When the hangman, Pierpont, arrived to confront him for the last time he walked steadily towards the noose that awaited him. The rope was actually around his hempen neck before he came wide awake and started to shout.

'Stop! Oh, God, forgive me—'

But by then Pierpont had pulled the lever of the drop, and the killer of William Edward Hall dropped to eternity.

2

EGYPT

Over the Garden Wall

Back in those days when Egypt was a country still to achieve the aspirations men sum up in the emotive word 'independence', a man who had already acquired considerable wealth was a certain Max Karam. He was a merchant who had been born in Syria and was the owner of a large home on the coast outside Alexandria. He lived in a studied and ostentatious style that could be described as near-Oriental. He was by nature industrious and shrewd and was proud of what he had achieved; one of his proudest possessions, as he thought of her, was his lovely wife.

However, if the truth were known, he was even prouder of his British nationality. For being British in that day and age held tremendous advantages. But in the nature of mysteries he was never to know one of them. It was the advantage of having competent British medico-legal minds tackle the problem imposed by one's murder.

The mystery was announced by Katina, a young Egyptian maid who knocked twice and received no customary reply, so tapped more loudly for the third time. It was about twenty minutes to nine o'clock. She turned the handle of the door and entered Max Karam's wide bedroom. A few feet inside the room she pulled up short and stared.

Her master appeared to be sitting by the bed, and at first she thought he was asleep. He was in an almost sitting position. His legs were thrust out before him, with one hand overlaying the other, almost in an attitude of prayer. His mouth was closed, and he appeared to be pouting in his sleep, for his eyes were almost closed.

But there was no movement. His thickset body did not rise and fall with breathing, and no sound came from those pouting lips. The maid stared in bewildered fascination, and then it was that the truth slowly filled her with a grisly horror. She knew that Karam was dead.

The cream mosquito net was a soft wave of broken foam that had been torn from its rails over the tumbled bed and was now entwined around the squatting man's enveloped corpse. Only death could explain the overturned commode which appeared to be propped up on the outstretched legs. The lamp that normally stood on the commode had fallen to the floor some distance away.

If the suddenly frightened girl had doubts, or if the thought crossed her mind that her master had been taken ill and had collapsed when trying to get out of bed, sight of the blood on his nightshirt resolved them. Stifling her fear, she tiptoed closer and put out a timid hand to touch the seated corpse. The flesh was cold.

She stooped to move a limb, but found it rigid; she remained in her stooping position, her wide eyes staring at what appeared to be a brown scorch mark on the right sleeve of the nightshirt. It couldn't make sense to her mind in its upset state at the discovery. Suddenly of her own volition she rose and gave a piercing scream.

The sound stilled suddenly as she thought to take herself in hand. She turned and hurried from the room. As she closed the door of that room of death she began calling loudly, awakening the household. Within minutes the local police were speeding to the large house by the Mediterranean. The date was January 15th, 1923.

The Egyptian police, who had been trained by British officers, began a competent inquiry into a crime they quickly established as murder. They found a drying pool of blood on the mattress of the bed with the ripped-away mosquito netting, which was dappled with blood splotches and in places had similar scorch marks to that on the sleeve of the dead man's nightshirt. Only inches from the tacky pool of blood in the bed was a bunch of keys on a steel ring.

Karam's nightly habit had been to place that bunch of keys under his pillow. It had been a precaution he had taken for many years. One of the keys in the bunch opened the safe in his shore home. In that safe was normally kept a considerable sum in cash as well as some valuable pieces of jewellery. However, when the key was turned in the safe's door both money and jewellery were in their accustomed places. The dead man had not been robbed. Indeed, if robbery had been the motive the murderer had gone empty-handed from the scene of his crime.

The dead man had been beaten about the head, although this had not been readily apparent at first glance. High on the head were lacerations running parallel to one another, and from both their direction and position it seemed that Max Karam had been struck while confronting his killer. The murder weapon had been dropped or thrown away. It had fallen between the reclining corpse and the bed. It was an iron bar about eighteen inches long. More of Karam's tacky blood adhered to one end of it, like a repulsive jelly that was turning black when the police examined it.

However, although the safe had not been opened, it appeared that an attempt had been made to force open the door of a stout wooden cupboard. Clear jemmy marks had been made in the edge of the door, in an attempt to prise it open. But the lock had held, and the door had not been successfully forced apart.

This was the sum total of what the bedroom had to yield to the search by the police. It was, to say the least, puzzling. From the bedroom the police turned their attention to the other rooms in the large house where women could be heard crying softly. They found, on the ground floor, a door with a hole in it that was oval in shape, and easily recognized by professional police eyes. The hole was approximately six inches long by half that across, and had been made by drilling a number of much smaller holes with a brace and bit and then breaking loose from the door the central piece these holes had ringed. The method was one used by professional burglars in the Near East.

Outside the door with the oval hole lay a small pile of sawdust and wood turnings on the floor. A few inches away was the serrated central piece of wood that had been tugged loose to allow the entry of a hand, which had reached the inside bolt. This had been secured in a wall slot and held in place by a short chain which ran through a steel ring. It was a strange contraption, but should have proved effective against mere force in opening the door.

To the police this appeared to be a most curious discovery. For the person who had cut out the piece of the door by using a brace and bit had known where to start drilling to be sure of being able to reach the chain and the bolt and the ringed chain. Such a person was obviously no stranger to the household on the shore.

In support of this were severed wires of the electric alarm system. The wires that ran to the alarm bell had been cut, although the wires had been cunningly concealed in the wall. Actually the electric wires had been cut on both sides of the house, so that even the bells in the kitchen had been put out of action. This thorough job had been completed when the telephone line had been severed.

The police were immediately suspicious of such a complete attempt to deceive them, as they considered. Their reaction was to suspect some member of the dead man's household of having killed him and then of having drilled the hole in the door and cut the telephone and electric bell wires to make it appear that an outsider had forced an entry.

If the police theory required any additional support it was supplied by the fact that a night watchman was employed to watch over the household during the hours of darkness. But this man had seen and heard nothing. This seemed to point to his movements being timed and known.

After completing their search the police returned to the room where the tearful widow awaited them. She was no longer crying, but gave visible signs of being acutely distressed. However, she endeavoured to compose herself sufficiently to answer a string of probing questions between choked silences. She explained that on the previous night her husband had given a dinner party, specially arranged for some friends. The party had ended about midnight, as near as she could remember. Her husband had seen his guests leave, and afterwards the night watchman had been told to go round and check the securing of doors and windows in his usual custom. When her husband had turned to go up to his own bedroom she had accompanied him.

She told the police, 'I remained in his bedroom for about half an hour.'

'How did he seem to you?' asked the senior police officer in a tone suggesting that the question might have special relevance.

Her reply was prompt.

'He was very happy. He continued talking about the party and our guests.' The widow nodded as though to emphasize something. 'He said he had enjoyed our friends coming and made a few jokes.'

'Then you would say he was in very good spirits, Mrs Karam?'

'Oh, yes, most certainly,' said the widow without any hesitation.

'Then it would be true to say that your husband did not appear to you like a man who was expecting trouble from any source?'

'Trouble?' asked the widow, wide-eyed and perplexed. 'Why, no. Nothing seemed farther from his mind. Why should he expect trouble?'

'He was murdered,' the senior police officer reminded her.

However, the police were there to ask questions, not to answer them, and the questions continued until the woman explained how she had been kissed good-night by Max Karam, and had then left his room to go to her own, which was some distance along a passage and was separated from her husband's by two intervening rooms.

Then she went on to explain how, as was usual with her, she had fallen asleep almost as soon as she had climbed into bed. That would have been shortly before one o'clock, as near as she could tell, for she had not thought to look at the time. But it was later that she was roused by a sound like a heavy thud, as though some weighty object had fallen. But she was half asleep at the time. She could not say where the noise had come from; it seemed to have come from somewhere in the house, although she could not say precisely where, and remained listening for some time, and concluded, in her half-awake state, that she must have been dreaming. She had accordingly turned over, closed her eyes, and gone back to sleep.

The next thing she remembered was being awakened by Katina. That was about half-past six, her normal time for rising each morning.

'I thought I heard a noise in the middle of the night,' she told the girl. 'Like a thump, Katina. You didn't hear it, I suppose?'

To her surprise the girl said she had.

'Yes, madame,' said Katina, 'I did hear a heavy sort of thud, but it didn't go on. I thought it must have been a shutter that had banged in the wind and then snapped shut, as they do sometimes.'

'We'll go and see, Katina,' the mistress told her maid.

She put on some clothes, and the pair went downstairs to look around the ground floor. By this time it was daylight and the night watchman had left. Mrs Karam's hurried examination of the ground-floor rooms revealed nothing out of place, and she returned to her own room, not wanting to disturb her husband.

She was in that wing of the house when later Katina's cry of alarm rang through the rooms. The maid had a much better idea of the time of the heavy thud than her mistress.

'It was about three o'clock,' she told the police quite positively.

However, the other servants in the large establishment had nothing to tell which offered a clue or reason for the violence and apparent forceful entry. The night watchman was also questioned. He was plainly scared, but apparently telling the truth when he insisted that he had heard nothing during the night.

The police made a thorough examination of the garden surrounding the sprawling house, and they came upon a gap among the iron spikes of a *chevaux de frise* topping the boundary wall. The missing iron spike was found on the ground on the other side of the wall. It had seemingly been broken off by an unknown tugging at it. From below the space left by the missing spike, on the inside of the long wall, ran footprints in the soft earth. These led straight to the house, and detectives took plaster casts of several of the prints. They were compared with footprints made by various members of the Karam household. But the trail of prints provided no matching pair, and the police found themselves baffled.

They had to do some rethinking, not necessarily to change their ideas about the crime and its commission, but certainly to include some additional possibilities.

In the meantime the body of the murdered man was removed to a mortuary in the town, and some time later a post-mortem was undertaken by a medical officer attached to the British Consulate in Alexandria. The murdered Max Karam was being given the final service due to him as a man of British nationality, of which in life he had been so inordinately proud.

The medical official was somewhat surprised to find that the dead man, aged somewhere in his early forties, had been such a splendid physical specimen. Karam, in fact, had been a man of powerful physique, and had certainly not been a man an intruder would tackle lightly if challenged. The chances are he would have been stronger than his opponent.

But one piece of mystery was cleared up when it was proved that Karam had suffered a dual attack.

The three wounds already observed by the police were traced across the vertex, front to back, without the doctor finding that the skull had been fractured. But the powder burns on the right sleeve of his nightshirt and in the mosquito netting pointed to a gunshot, and the wound was followed from a puncture below the left eyelid to an entry below the right ear and a little behind it.

The bullet which had been fired into the back of Karam's head in such a cowardly fashion had penetrated the victim's brain. But curiously there were no powder burns at the back of the head, and the short hairs in the nape of the neck and around the ear did not have that distinctive burned-powder smell. The police believed that the bullet had been fired from some distance.

In the post-mortem the cap of skull was removed and dissected from the covering of the holed brain, which had marked haemorrhage on its moist surface. Indeed, the bullet's passage was now clear. It had travelled at right angles to the surface of the skull, splintering the base with fissured fractures and damaging the sphenoid bone.

The medical man's forceps removed a couple of cartridge wads and a copper-covered bullet from the hole in the punctured brain. There was every appearance of Max Karam having been shot dead.

In that case, why the superficial wounds caused by the iron bar that had been found close to the bed?

This imposed an unanswered mystery.

The local police, confronted by the results of the post-mortem, admitted they were puzzled, but they still clung to their theory that the murder had been committed by someone in the dead man's own household. At least, it was a theory that covered most of the known facts, though by no means all of them.

A discussion at the British Consulate resulted in a suggestion that the local Alexandria police were not reluctant to avail themselves of, for the case, as one of murder, was presented formally to the experts of the Medico-Legal Department in Cairo, which was staffed with British officers.

So a fresh investigation was begun.

A new theory produced a fresh consideration of the known facts and relevant factors. It was finally decided that Karam had not been shot by someone inside his own household. Instead, the signs were that the murderer had come from outside, and certainly the killer had been no novice at forceful entry as the use of a brace and bit showed all too clearly.

Further, the British members of the Medico-Legal Department found no trace of fingerprints on surfaces that could be expected to retain them. This suggested the killer, or even possibly killers, had worn gloves. In short, the murder had been a professional job. This, too, was supported by a fresh examination of the blood-smeared iron bar that had been found in the master bedroom. It was shaped like a conventional jemmy, with a tapering point at one end and a curved claw at the other for easy levering. It was most likely to be the jemmy used unsuccessfully on the stout timbers of the strong wooden cupboard.

The jemmy went under the microscope. Traces of brass and chalk were found in some of the irregularities in the metal's surfaces close to the ends. The blood on it was tested, and found to be one of the same group as Karam's. Fibrous particles adhering to the jemmy proved to be of the same substance as the cream mosquito netting.

It was decided after further careful consideration that the bullet must have been fired when the mosquito net was drawn, and with the gun held close to the netting. Additional calculations suggested that Karam was not lying prone in his bed at the time of the shot, but was actually sitting upright, perhaps with his feet out of the bed, but certainly swathed in the mosquito net, which had not been drawn back.

Moreover, these calculations pointed specifically to the victim's right arm being raised to afford protection for his head. In this way, the nightshirt sleeve had been scorched together with the netting over his head. But at the same time Karam must have been facing a person who had struck him with the jemmy from in front.

The suggestion was now clear that one person had attacked the victim with a gun in the rear, while another had moved in to deal with him in front, wielding the jemmy. This meant two attackers. The one behind had moved to shoot from the right.

This could mean a pair of known professional burglars, who had carefully acquired knowledge of how the household was run and of its security aspects. If this was indeed so, it was well-nigh certain that the attackers had entered through the forced downstairs door, crossed the ground floor to the wide marble staircase, and then crept up to the first floor. They had done this without disturbing the night watchman, so they had moved silently.

On the first floor the staircase branched off in two directions, the first towards the master bedroom and Max Karam's suite of rooms, the second towards another suite, occupied by Karam's brother and the latter's wife.

The bell wires from each suite had been severed.

Having established how the murder had been committed, the detectives from the Medico-Legal Department in Cairo turned their attention to the problem of why. They started with the safe which, presumably, had been the thieves' target—always supposing that theft had been the true motive for entry and the ensuing murder.

It was a wall-safe built into the small dressing-room that adjoined Mrs Karam's bedroom. As no attempt had been made to force the safe, it was believed that the thieves must have known, among other details of the household arrangements, that Karam habitually slept at night with his keys under his pillow. The procedure they had followed was likely to be—first cutting the bell wires and the telephone line, then stealing to Karam's room to try working the bunch of keys from under the sleeping man's head. Karam could be expected to be sleeping like a log after the late party.

But Karam had wakened and immediately turned on his attackers and was promptly hit over the head by the man holding the jemmy. There had been no light in the room, and Karam had been a shadow entwined in the mosquito netting. Moreover, he had been a man of considerable strength. The blows had not stunned him. Whereupon the second man had quickly shot him in the head.

The intruders had thereupon panicked completely and run from the house.

At a conference the Alexandria police accepted both the theory and the tentative reconstruction of the crime. They soon began pulling in known professional burglars for questioning. At this point the widow came forward with an offer of two thousand pounds' reward for information that would lead to the arrest and conviction of the culprits.

The result of this precipitate announcement was for a motley army of persons to come forward with a host of suggestions, among which only a very few withstood the first few shrewd police questions.

But it took three weeks to eliminate all such hopeful clues, and the murder case was growing stale before, some twenty days from the crime, someone talked. She was a Frenchwoman of the European paved streets who was known to her clientèle as Henriette. She called at the police station and said somewhat defiantly, 'I have something to tell you about the Karam mystery.'

According to her story she had been living with a German. This man had another German friend named Ferid Merkel, but Henriette said she was sure this was not the man's rightful name. Merkel liked the bottle, and when he had imbibed enough he became talkative. She had heard him speaking to the German she lived with about a burglary he and another man had undertaken. After listening to their conversation for some time Henriette realized Merkel was boasting about participating in the Karam killing. At first she had been scared.

But when she read of the reward that had been offered by the widow she decided the time had come when she had to think for herself and of her own position.

'If Merkel finds out I have been to the police,' she said with a shudder that was genuine, 'he'll open me with a knife. I shall want protection as well as a reward,' she added fearfully.

She was told to go home and say nothing, but to act normally. Detectives set out to examine Merkel's lodging, where he lived with another man when the place was unoccupied. The police searchers came away with some burglar's tools and a pair of well-worn gloves. Among the former were a brace and bit, which were dispatched for examination by the Medico-Legal Department. The bit was found to be of the same size as that which had made the drilled holes in the villa's door. Particles of brown paint were found in the teeth of one of the files among the tools. This matched the paint on the forced door. The ends of the worn gloves were smeared with a chalky substance that was tested and proved to be limestone of similar quality and texture as that with which some of the Karam villa's walls had been lime-washed.

The detectives going through the Merkel lodging came upon a blue serge suit, in the jacket pocket of which they found gritty particles of sand and limestone as well as some small wood chips, a piece of rusty iron, a bit of jagged glass, and a small piece of plaster.

The wood chips had been taken from the forced villa door as comparison of both grain and cutting shape revealed, and the small piece of plaster could possibly have come from the Karam home.

One of the more interesting articles discovered at the lodging was a visiting card with the name of Klaus Chefer. It was with a morocco jewel case that was empty and some toothpicks that had been taken from the Petrograd Restaurant in Cairo. In a drawer were found two photographs of women. One bore the photographer's name — Robert Hanneman, Leipzig. This one had stains around the edges and small holes at the top, where a nail had held it on a wall. The woman in the other photograph was older and did not look Nordic. Her photo had been taken at the London Studio, Cairo.

The laboratory of the Medico-Legal Department established that fair hairs taken from a brush and comb in the lodging had atrophied roots, which meant that the head those hairs had come from was going bald. On the other hand, hairs taken from a felt hat and from the collar of the blue serge suit were much longer and almost black. But among the long dark hairs on the jacket collar was one fair hair of shoulder length—a woman's. It didn't take the detectives long to learn that Merkel was short and stumpy, fair and balding, while his fellow-lodger, whose real name was Klauss, was taller with dark hair. Klaus Chefer was in fact Klauss, while Ferid Merkel was really a man named Doelitzsch.

Inquiries were made at the German Embassy, where an interesting story was unfolded of two German sailors who on the 31st of January had reported meeting another German in Alexandria on the 18th. He had said he was Herman Klauss and living under the name of Klaus Chefer. He had invited them to visit him aboard the *Valtamery*, moored in the harbour, and boasted of a burglary he had pulled up the coast with a man named Merkel. The German visitors realized they had been told about the Karam crime. They decided to report to their own embassy, but unfortunately since then the *Valtamery* had sailed through the Suez Canal for India.

The Egyptian police cabled the Indian police and eventually a Magnus Klausen was returned to Egypt on April 13th, but claimed he was not Herman Klauss under another name. However, the mystery was resolved when an Indian sergeant who had travelled with Klausen recognized the wanted Klauss, when shown the German's photo, as a man in jail in Calcutta, arrested for jumping ship. It took more weeks, but finally Klauss was brought back to Egypt, by which time Merkel had been traced to Germany after an embassy secretary had recognized Merkel as a sailor named Fritz Doelitzsch who had signed on aboard the *Georgia*, on the 29th of January, a week before Henriette had gone to the police. The *Georgia* was traced to Trieste, where the police wired the Italian Consulate in Alexandria. Following exchanged wires the wanted man was soon in custody, again bound for Egypt, where the mystery was sorted out in Cairo.

While the sailors admitted the burglary, they denied killing Karam at the villa. They said they had first gone to the villa on the night of January 13th, but had been scared by an armed patrol, and had returned the next night, scaled the garden wall, breaking off one of the iron spikes, and had bored a hole through the house door. But at the trial no one explained how they came to know where precisely to drill the hole or to cut the wires. They said they had found money in a vase and a locked chest which they could not force open. Doelitzsch, gun in hand, and Klauss gripping a jemmy, had mounted to the next floor, where they parted company and exchanged weapons, or so they claimed. But Klauss backed into a chair and toppled a large vase, awakening Karam, who grappled with a figure seen through the mosquito net. In self-defence Doelitzsch had struck Karam over the head as Klauss ran into the shadowy room, firing from the right, and Doelitzsch had dropped the jemmy and run, arriving at their lodging about half-past five.

But Klauss told a different story, claiming that it was only after reaching the ground floor that he had heard the gunshot and that he had passed to his confederate both weapons, which seemed extremely unlikely.

Unfortunately for Klauss, the more glib of the pair, the reconstruction of the crime made by the Medico-Legal Department's experts was accepted by the court, which meant both men had struck the victim, and the prosecution claimed premeditation because the burglars had come armed and had stopped to fight with the awakened Karam instead of decamping.

However, when all the various pleas were on record and all the evidence had been submitted, the only question remaining was the paramount one of who fired the single shot?

Because there could be no outright proof, the court found both men guilty of the murder and sentenced each to penal servitude for life.

3

AMERICA

The Mystery of the Flying Blood

One of the strangest mysteries of America in the 'fifties was undoubtedly that of the man most Americans thought of as Dr Sam after his incredible story had received coast-to-coast publicity. It had resulted in two widely reported trials of sensational interest for the murder of his wife Marilyn. At least one major film had been made of the story and several books written about the mystery, and today, years after Sam Sheppard's death, there are many who feel that the last word has not been said on the subject of what happened on a very windy day in July 1954.

It was July 3rd when Dr Sheppard, a popular man of considerable personal charm as well as professional standing as an osteopath among the people of Bay Village, a small community on the shores of Lake Erie, decided to mark the forthcoming 4th of July celebrations with a party for his friends the Aherns. The visitors consisted of Don Ahern and his wife Nancy and their children. Like the Sheppards they lived only a short distance away in West Lake Road, where their garden plot ran down to a private beach.

It was decided that the Aherns should come to the Sheppards as Dr Sam, as everyone called him familiarly, had to attend a call at the local hospital and couldn't get away again for about an hour. The womenfolk elected to get dinner and wait for him.

The Aherns arrived at about six o'clock, when Marilyn told Chip, the Sheppards' young son of six, to go out and play with the Ahern children, leaving the adults to their drinks and gossip.

They all seemed relaxed. Later the two women finished preparing a summer meal while their husbands sauntered down to the nearby beach after Sam had returned from his hospital visit.

'These white-caps won't make it very smooth for skiing across the lake,' Sam Sheppard mused, watching curling breakers washing the sand bordering a steep embankment. 'There's another hospital picnic fixed for tomorrow, and if this wind keeps up I don't fancy their chances for a ski run.'

Ahern agreed.

'That's the best of sticking to golf,' he grinned. 'At least you can't drown.'

When dinner was announced Don Ahern collected his children and took them home to put them to bed. Then he returned to the women and Dr Sam and the two couples settled down in the comfortable lounge. Chip had already been put to bed. Sheppard switched on the television and tuned to a film, but his eyes drooped. He had performed a tricky operation earlier and felt sleepy. His head slipped back on the couch. The film ended at twelve-thirty and Marilyn, who was four months pregnant, felt as tired as Sam looked.

'I can hardly keep my eyes open,' she apologized to the Aherns.

'Well, it's high time we were making tracks,' said Nancy. 'I'll just look in on the children—oh, and that reminds me, Marilyn,' she went on. 'Make sure you latch and chain the front door. One can't be too careful about taking precautions, as I keep telling Don.'

Marilyn nodded and said goodnight to her guests, patted her mouth to smother a yawn, and then stood waving to them as she closed the front door. The latch clicked and she switched off the light.

Five hours later a 'phone rang in the home of Bay Village's mayor, Spencer Houk, which was only three houses away from the Sheppard residence.

He woke and scowled at the insistent instrument and threw back the bedclothes.

'Who the devil is it at this hour?' he demanded irritably.

A voice he could only with difficulty recognize as Sam Sheppard's called urgently, 'Get over here quick, Spence. My God, they've killed Marilyn!'

'Who—what—' the roused mayor stammered and broke off, for Sheppard had already slammed down the receiver and the only sound was the broken bleeping of the familiar dialling tone.

His wife had already been roused, and the pair, now wide awake, hurriedly scrambled into their clothes and in little more than ten minutes arrived at the Sheppards' front door, which they found unlocked and wide. It was first light, and on the floor of the hall the mayor saw a doctor's bag which had been upended with its contents spilled across the carpet. Sam Sheppard was slumped down in an easy chair by a desk in his den.

'What's this all about, Sam?' inquired the mayor, looking at his wife in puzzlement.

Sheppard groaned, shaking his head.

'I don't know,' he said, the words clearing. 'But someone ought to look at Marilyn.'

Esther Houk climbed the stairs to the first floor, while her husband was taking stock of observable details. Three drawers from the desk had been stacked on the floor and Sam Sheppard was clad only in socks, shoes, and slacks. His torso was bare. As he stepped into the living-room Houk glimpsed a tan corduroy jacket on a settee or couch and saw that the drawers of another desk had been pulled out and a pile of papers was strewn across the floor.

He was interrupted by his wife's hurrying feet on the stairs.

'Get the police!' she called. 'And get an ambulance—only hurry!'

The mayor snatched up the 'phone and alerted the police. He then rang Dr Richard Sheppard, Sam's eldest brother, who lived only a short distance away. Uniformed officers were quickly at the scene, and the mayor accompanied them to the bedroom at the top of the stairs, where they found Marilyn lying battered in a blood-soaked bed. More than a dozen heavy blows had smashed her skull, destroying her head. Her face, arms, and upper body had also been bludgeoned. She was sprawled on her back, with her legs dangling over the bed's foot. A stained sheet partly covered the remains. The body was clad in pyjamas, one leg free of the trousers and the top tugged down. There was a copious amount of blood. The brother of Dr Sam took only a few moments to inform the police that his sister-in-law was dead. He was clearly shocked by the brutality of the crime, which was destined to become one of the most notorious mysteries of the age.

Meantime, Dr Sam had collapsed and was removed to hospital, while young Chip, who had slept through his mother's murder, was dressed and hurriedly taken to the home of another of the Sheppard brothers, Dr Stephen Sheppard.

Then the police began their questioning. They heard from the Aherns of the informal party which continued until after midnight, when Nancy Ahern herself secured the door into the yard on the Lake Erie side of the house.

'Marilyn was asleep on her feet. In fact, they both were,' she admitted. 'I believe Sam went to sleep on the couch, which was why Marilyn didn't waken him. He was bushed after a long day at the hospital.'

Dr Sam, the Aherns said, had gone home wearing a white T-shirt, slacks, and the corduroy jacket. They said he was frequently sleepy and given to dozing because of his long hours in the hospital. To the police, after listening to the Aherns' story, it seemed a case of a burglar being disturbed by Marilyn Sheppard and being viciously struck down to prevent an alarm being raised. But a rational enlargement suggested that Dr Sam had been awakened by his wife. He then ran to her aid and was struck down by the intruder, who was by then anxious only to escape.

The coroner agreed with the enlargement when the husband explained that he had been awakened by his wife's cries of 'Sam! Sam!' He had rushed upstairs and was met by a blow on the back of the head.

'I was rendered unconscious,' he told Dr Samuel Gerber.

He had no idea how long he remained unconscious, but it could not have been long for he came to when he heard a noise in the living-room and ran back downstairs in time to see what he said was 'a form' running towards the disturbed waters of the lake. He gave chase to a beach hut where he confronted the mystery man. They struggled and he was knocked down, losing consciousness again and coming to with his face in the lake and his legs in deeper water. When he collected his scattered wits he groped his way back to the house, climbed the stairs, and discovered the horror of the battered Marilyn.

He could hardly credit what had happened and he was incoherent when he rang Houk, but he could not say how long had passed in that wild interval. Later he varied his dramatic story. He told a couple of Cleveland detectives from his hospital bed on the Sunday morning that he now thought there had been two intruders, one who attacked Marilyn Sheppard and a second man who had hammered himself. While recovering consciousness at the head of the stairs he saw his wallet on the floor. In it were three dollar bills and three twenty-dollar notes. When the detectives withdrew he lay listening to the noises of a typical Fourth of July Sunday when everyone seemed to be *en fête*, except the doctor who had lost a wife. His head ached and he fell asleep.

It was Larry Houk, the mayor's son, who made an early find. In some scrub not far from the lake he came upon a green bag containing Dr Sam's automatic winding watch. There were several water drops under the wrist-watch's glass and several dried spots of blood on the band. The green bag, which usually held tools for the doctor's outboard motor, also contained his key-chain and signet ring. The contents of this bag had been spilled on to the floor of the den in the Sheppards' home, and among them lay

Marilyn's watch, stained with blood. There was more money in the den and other sums in an upstairs room.

But one seeming discrepancy puzzled the police. The Aherns had reported that Sam Sheppard had gone to sleep wearing a T-shirt under his tan jacket. But when he summoned the Houks he had been stripped naked from the waist up. The corduroy jacket had been neatly folded on the couch.

The detectives broadened their inquiries, but did so discreetly. They had learned that Sam and Marilyn Sheppard had been childhood sweethearts, but that a red-headed hospital technician called Susan Hayes had attracted the doctor's roving eye until she had left Bay Village in February to secure a post in Los Angeles. A month later the Sheppards journeyed to California to attend an osteopathic convention Dr Sam felt was important to his career. But when Sheppard said he had not indulged in an affair with the redhead, it was Susan Hayes who revealed that she had spent a week with him in Los Angeles while Marilyn was staying with another doctor's family near Oakland, some four hundred miles away. Sheppard had bought a watch for the redhead to replace one she had lost at a wedding party attended by both of them. He had also bought her a ring, and she said she had been Dr Sam's lover for more than a year.

While the threads of the Sheppard episode in California were being woven and taking shape Detectives Schottke and Careau in Cleveland were getting down to further details. They asked Sheppard how badly he had been hurt.

'My brother can tell you,' said the man whose wife had been murdered brutally. 'I'm told that my neck is broken.'

Stephen Sheppard said that an X-ray plate revealed that a vertebrae joint in his brother's neck was chipped and that he was suffering from shock and bruises.

'It is possible,' he told the police, 'that he has suffered brain injury.'

At the best it wasn't conclusive.

The post-mortem had given the time of death as somewhere between three and four in the morning, and Sheppard's self-winding watch had stopped at four-fifteen. On the Monday the Cleveland pair returned to ask the man in the hospital bed if he could recall any further details of the man he had chased towards the lake.

Sheppard shook his head and said, 'Only that he was a biggish man with bushy hair.'

Stephen Sheppard came into the room at this point. He looked serious as he informed his listeners that he had retained counsel for his brother.

'So I can't allow you to ask any further questions,' he told the detectives, who shared a glance and withdrew in silence.

A few days later Sheppard, wearing a surgical collar, left the hospital to attend his wife's funeral; he avoided both Press and police. In fact his avoidance of anything in the nature of news or publicity so annoyed the coroner that Gerber threatened him with a subpoena. Possibly due to this on July 10th Sam Sheppard signed a nine-page formal statement in which he stated that his wife 'may have tried to awaken him and get him to go to bed'. But he was not sure, he said, for he remained on the couch, until he was roused by her cries and heard her moaning. He ran upstairs, sure that she was suffering from a convulsion of the sort she had had in the early days of her pregnancy. But then he was given a blow on the head, which rendered him unconscious until he came to beside Marilyn's bed.

'I looked at my wife,' he related. 'I believe I felt her pulse and felt that she was gone.'

He looked into Chip's room and found him still sleeping, but when he heard a noise downstairs he turned and gave chase. However, the man landed a blow that knocked the doctor out.

Probed about the Sheppards' home life, he claimed it was ideal and firmly denied ever becoming enraged and angry with Marilyn when discussing what he called marital problems. All the same, it was obvious that the questions were becoming more pointed and penetrating the longer the process of asking and answering continued.

'Do you know of any reason why someone else would take her life?' was one rapier-like thrust from which Sheppard flinched visibly.

He wiped his mouth.

'Possibly,' he said uncertainly. 'I have heard of individuals who are maniacal enough that when they start something, an act like that, it becomes a compulsion.' Then more certainly he added, 'She has spurned lovers, potential lovers.'

There was sudden silence while the coroner considered what had been said.

'How many of these potential lovers did she have?'

'Three I know of, and I am pretty sure more. I am certain that there were more.'

While notes were being transcribed he suddenly seemed to take a mental plunge. He named three men. One was Spencer Houk, a second was Dr Hoversten, and the third a distant relative of Marilyn Sheppard. The unravelling threads explained, at least partially, several new facts. For instance, on the 3rd of July it was established that Sam Sheppard had been both preoccupied and morose, but on the 4th, the day of the murder, Dr Hoversten had hastened to Bay Village to express his commiseration with the appalling news of the tragedy. The police had quietly checked his alibi. It could not be faulted. Nor could the alibis of both Houk and Marilyn's relative.

By this time the police were indulging in fresh thoughts about the crime, and a growing query was expressed by them about the possible motive of a husband who could have slaughtered his wife so brutally. For one thing was not explained away. Why had someone apparently taken the trouble to remove so many smudged fingerprints in the Sheppards' home? Who was incriminated and why was a trail of blood cleaned up, howbeit not very thoroughly?

After a further discussion with the police and Dr Gerber the latter announced that a formal inquest would be heard on the 22nd of July. By this time the case was accumulating vast public interest throughout the Middle West, and Sam Sheppard swore on oath that he had not been guilty of murdering his wife nor had he indulged in a love affair with Susan Hayes.

But there was, the police learned, evidence to refute this latter claim and the story of Sheppard's week spent in Susan Hayes's company and the watch lost at a wedding party became current news. The case widened into the dimensions of a *cause célèbre* when Sam Sheppard was arrested for murder and charged. Then began a three-month period before the hearing of the trial in October 1954. The police were busy checking on likely clues, 'To sew up the case,' as the District Attorney explained to impatient newsmen.

However, there was a good deal of speculation about the merits of the case, and a good many people believed that the popular Dr Sam would be able to clear his name of all imputation in the sordid crime, and as month followed month into the autumn the arguments as to the complicity or otherwise of the doctor grew more voluble and heated.

At last, with the concentrated and riveted gaze of America on the figure of Dr Sam seated at his counsel's table, the trial opened on the 18th of October. The court was crowded to hear the opening words by Judge Edward Blythin, but it did not take long for the first dramatic development. It was provided by the prosecution's first witness, who was Dr Lester Adelson, the deputy coroner. He began by showing a series of colour slides on a screen, including photographs of the terrible wounds inflicted on the victim's smashed head.

They brought an audible gasp from the persons in court, who after showing their revulsion turned to stare at the defendant. Sam Sheppard's shoulders were seen to quiver and tremble beneath the fabric of his neat blue serge. He resolutely turned his gaze away from the slides. Seconds later he broke into convulsive sobbing. But Dr Adelson continued and paid no attention to the side-drama. Using a ruler, he pointed out the thirty-five wounds for the jurors' benefit as he admitted there had been no sex attack on the victim, but turned to declare that 'the cause of death is plain enough'.

There was utter silence in the court.

Sheppard's counsel, Attorney William J. Corrigan, rose to cross-examine the witness and a wrangle ensued. Adelson admitted that there had been no microscopic study of the various wounds, neither had there been a toxicologist's examination of the victim's internal organs. He made the point that seven gashes in her forehead were just one inch apart and parallel, and he developed the argument that death had been caused by a seven-pronged instrument, and then he insinuated that Marilyn could have been poisoned, and even that she might have drowned in her own blood.

By this time the court was sitting erect.

'It's all circumstantial,' he declared waspishly, and said he intended to question every statement made by the prosecution.

The spectators settled down for an intensive session.

Attorney Corrigan claimed he knew what the murder weapon was, but was careful not to define it; he said that a four-month-old male foetus taken from Marilyn's body was not buried with her, but possibly it was for further use in the examination. The cross-examination ground on.

So did the arguments.

For instance, the prosecution insisted that if Sheppard had indeed been knocked out and left unconscious on the beach on a night of growing storm conditions, he would have drowned. But it was Spencer Houk's telling of the 'phone call that produced a real surprise. He claimed that when Richard Sheppard first told Sam that Marilyn was dead the elder brother asked a curious question.

'He said either, "Did you do this?" or "Did you have anything to do with this?" and Sam replied, "Hell, no!" ' Houk told the court.

He also claimed that on the day before the inquest he said to Sheppard, 'If you did this crime come out and say you did. If it was done by you, it was done in a fit of rage. If you did it, all your family and friends will be behind you.'

Sheppard's reply was a dogged, 'I couldn't have done it.'

However, the defence attorney mounted a special attack on the coroner, whom he claimed had disregarded many clues pointing to Sheppard's innocence. But Dr Gerber came up with a surprise of his own and produced a ghoulish exhibit, a blood-stained pillow removed from the slain woman's bed. He said he had found an impression of a two-bladed instrument, which he said must have been the murder weapon. But the surgical instrument, or whatever it was, had been removed and the pillow turned over. But in contrast, Marilyn's wrist-watch had not been taken off until the blood had dried. In view of Sheppard's claim to have followed the intruder to the beach it seemed extremely unlikely that he would in the circumstances have removed his wife's watch and left it in the den. The case was assuming improbables. Also some snide remarks.

For instance, when Corrigan had asked of the coroner whether there had at any time been a projected divorce and he had replied, 'Yes, sir,' he had rejoined, 'Well, you're divorced, aren't you?'

There had been instant objection by the prosecutor.

'He was asking about divorce,' said Corrigan with mock-mildness.

'But his wife wasn't killed,' snapped the prosecutor.

'And Dr Sam didn't kill his wife,' shouted the defence attorney.

It was a ding-dong legal battle until Susan Hayes appeared, dressed demurely, and related events that occurred in California. She stated in a low voice that she had never seen Sheppard lose his temper, that she had always been aware that he was a married man, and that he only used the word 'love' in signing her letters, when he inscribed them, 'Love, Sam'. Corrigan took the legal bull by the horns and moved for a direct acquittal. But the motion was denied by the judge, and so Dr Stephen Sheppard took the stand as the first of the defence's witnesses, and said, 'Sam is the most level-headed one in our family. I have never seen him rise in anger. I have never seen him speak in any way to indicate that he had lost his head. As a child, when he got into arguments, he always refrained from fighting.'

He contested the prosecution's evidence at almost every turn, flatly denying that his brother's jacket had been carefully folded and placed on the couch. It had been flung down on the floor. He contended also that his brother had suffered a spinal contusion in his grappling with the intruder, and insisted that police photographs of his sister-in-law's body while on the bed showed both her clothing and an arm in postures and positions different from those he noted upon first seeing her and when he saw her a short time later.

However, on the following day he wavered in cross-examination. Thomas Parrino, the assistant prosecutor, forced him to admit that he had 'erred somewhat' in his testimony about the position of the body, but he hedged about the photographs and their actual position. His defensive stand was a prelude to the defendant taking the stand to give his own testimony, which the assembled court awaited with bated breath.

For here was the crux of mystery.

Would the defendant's testimony prove him to be innocent or otherwise?

Garbed in a dark grey suit with a white shirt, and wearing a sober-hued knitted tie, Dr Sam Sheppard turned and addressed his words to the jury. He spoke in a sequence of what many felt were stilted sentences and phrases interspersed with hesitant pauses, so that he cannot be said to have made the best impression on his listeners.

An example was when he referred to his hurry to bring help to his calling wife. The words he chose in such a threatening and dramatic moment fraught with danger sounded contrived and not spontaneous.

'I initiated an attempt,' he said, wiping dry lips, 'to gather enough senses to navigate the stairs.'

Small wonder the jury and other members of the court stared at him with a frown. It was as though he was speaking of a stranger. He told the court that his marriage had always been an ideal one and that he was a man who had welcomed his wife's second pregnancy, refuting all suggestion that he had not wanted the baby.

He was given some help at times by Attorney Corrigan in painting a glowing and warm picture of his marital life with a loving son and contented wife, whom he had no reason to harm. But Parrino, the assistant prosecutor, spoiled the effect of this picture. He asked a number of questions all directed to get Sheppard to admit that it was Marilyn's attacker whom he chased down the stairs and out of the house.

'I had that sensation,' was the way Sam Sheppard put it.

But Parrino wanted more than a sensation.

'Did you make any effort to get a weapon?' he demanded.

'No, sir.'

'Did you make an outcry?'

'I may have,' said Sheppard, hedging again. 'I don't know. I have never gone after anyone with a weapon.'

Suddenly Parrino changed direction.

'Isn't it a fact that you slapped your wife that morning?'

Again came the flat negative. 'No, sir.'

The assistant prosecutor slyly posed the next question to inquire expansively, 'After you killed her, Doctor, you rushed down those stairs, jumped from the platform on to the beach and fell and injured yourself?'

Sheppard reacted sharply.

'That is absolutely untrue and unfair!'

The needling went on, with the court seemingly mesmerized as were the jury, with the assistant prosecutor listing various items underlining the weaknesses in Sheppard's testimony, including the woman witness who had seen two lights on in the Sheppard home at a quarter past two in the morning of the crime. In rebuttal the defence stressed the defendant's injuries received during the struggle with the intruder, and eventually Judge Blythin summed up a difficult case and the jury filed out to consider their verdict.

They remained debating all aspects of it for a week before the foreman handed a folded paper to a court bailiff who duly offered it to the judge. All eyes were fixed on Edward Blythin as he read the slip of paper and started to read aloud: 'We, the jury, find the defendant not guilty of murder—'

There was a stir in court and Dr Sam was suddenly smiling. But the stirring was quelled and the smiling withered as the judge continued—'in the first degree, but guilty of murder in the second degree.'

There was a sound like an exhaled overcharged sigh.

Sam Sheppard's eyes went curiously blank, as though actual sight had left them as well as awareness. He made a choking sound, but no words came to his lips. A fearful anticlimax had already begun to set in. It was as though he was seeing a re-run of a secret truth that was not to be shared and must remain a mystery for all time.

Then the judge was speaking again, sentencing Sam Sheppard to imprisonment for life in the Ohio Penitentiary. There was a scramble and the reporters were suddenly busy at a line of telephones, for the trial had been snowballing in mounting interest.

But at last the longest-run trial in US legal history was over. The decision was to be argued to and fro, pro and con, for years, for whatever else the trial had proved it was to be considered inconclusive. But tragedy came to persons concerned with it. A month after Dr Sam was sentenced came the news that his mother had committed suicide. Shortly afterwards his father died. Death followed several other people connected with the case, and a member of the trial jury committed suicide, while until his death in 1961 William J. Corrigan maintained a legal fight to obtain his client's release.

The famous trial lawyer F. Lee Bailey stepped into the dead Corrigan's shoes, and in typical fighting form and fettle vowed he would earn for Sheppard a retrial, and his efforts were successful when the Supreme Court decided that such a hearing should take place as the previous trial had been prejudiced by an hysterical Press campaign.

It was on 24th October, 1966, almost a dozen years later, that Dr Sam arrived in court for yet another hearing to clear his name, and straight away the militant Lee Bailey went into the attack, claiming that there had never been an opportunity for fingerprints to be taken from the various items listed in the defendant's possession. But it was a medical technologist whose evidence gave Bailey pause for special consideration. She was Mary Cowan, who had examined the contents of the green bag at the time of the murder. She showed colour photographs to the court of the contents, and these photographs revealed Sheppard's watch as it was originally found, spotted with blood. Such spots, she informed the court, were made by 'flying blood'. Lee Bailey had a real task explaining the spots, especially when the prosecutor claimed that they must have got on to the watch while Sheppard was beating his wife to death.

Bailey spent days trying to overcome this evidence of 'flying blood'. He finally claimed there was further evidence of similar particles on the inside of the watch strap, which meant that they had got on to it after it had been removed from Sheppard's wrist. It was a clever legal interpretation and on November 16th, 1966, the fresh jury accepted his words, and Dr Sam Sheppard was duly found not guilty.

But by this time he was a broken man, both rejected and dejected in his former profession, and his marriage to his second wife, a divorcee, did not last long. He died in 1970.

4

FRANCE

An Insistence on Truth

One of the mysteries that qualify as a description of being one that is certainly stranger than fiction is a puzzle that occupied the minds of the French police shortly after the First World War. As a crime it was contemporary with the infamous Henri-Désiré Landru, whose head was struck from his shoulders by Anatole Deibler's guillotine in February 1922.

It was a crime with its own international elements, which made it unique, and it is, moreover, conceivable that the true mystery was concealed in sibling rivalry and distrust. There also remained a question mark against motive, and it certainly captured both the imagination and horror of the people of France, who have been indulged in an historical sharing of horrors, as well as violence in its many forms.

The story began shortly before the outbreak of war when the Paris police investigated a shooting incident in a flat in the rue de Sèvres; they decided it was a case of suicide. However, some sceptical people were not so easily satisfied as the detectives who called at No. 107 when they were summoned by the concierge. It was March 5th, 1914, and there was a hint of early spring in the air, the last spring Paris was to enjoy before the world became convulsed in an armed struggle that was to bring changes that made the easy-going days of that March seem like a gentle lull before a tropical storm.

But not in the flat in the rue de Sèvres.

There the detectives found Paul Jacques collapsed in a chair in the room he used as his study. A bullet had penetrated his right temple and the weapon from which the shot had been fired lay on the blood-stained carpet at his sprawled feet. The dead man was about twenty years older than his very distressed wife, who claimed that her maid Georgette Picourla had found the husband dead when she had taken him a cup of drinking chocolate. The police accepted this version of the story. It was not the truth. The discovery had been made not by the servant, who had been told by her mistress that Monsieur Jacques had shot himself, but—if it had been a discovery—by Madame Jacques herself. Had the police known this they might have taken longer to decide the cause of death.

Certainly the maid had doubts, but then she felt she had reason, for some weeks before she had observed her mistress tip a white powder from a packet into a tureen of soup specially prepared for the husband. Without telling Madame Jacques, the maid informed the husband of what she had seen. He had merely looked at her and nodded, but had taken a sample of the soup to a chemist he knew.

'I'd like this analysed—discreetly,' he said.

The chemist looked at the soup and his customer.

'Certainly, monsieur,' he agreed. Later he looked no more surprised when he informed Monsieur Jacques, 'It's a corrosive sublimate, and possibly lethal.'

Even Monsieur Jacques had not been surprised, but perhaps he had learned that he lived in the shadow of death. He had not seemed to care very much, which says a good deal for the kind of life he had led and lived with his younger wife.

When he had met her she was Hera Myrtel, a convent-educated young woman of charm and obvious breeding, the daughter of a Lyons tradesman of wealth and standing. She had been born in 1868, reared gently until her father's business enterprise crashed. She then went to Mexico, where at the age of twenty-four she captured the heart of an older man who was a silk merchant. She married Paul Jacques and returned to France with him. They settled in Paris, where their daughter Paule was born and the mother wrote romantic novels under her maiden name. Under the same name she published some verse. In time she gained a minor literary reputation, and because her husband had the money to indulge her whims and caprices she was able to establish a literary salon of sorts, where she met a number of the literary hangers-on to the coat-tails of those who have arrived. Quite a few were men, and some of them young and attractive and quite unscrupulous.

Hera Jacques found it a simple matter to indulge herself with a whole series of lovers, who came like perching rooks and disappeared the same way. If the silk merchant protested there is no record, because any protest was utterly ineffective. Paul Jacques was indulgent to a degree that was almost morbid. It was as though his pen-wielding wife could crush him by a mere show of contempt.

So perhaps he did not object to death as an eventual way out of a sickening dilemma he had no way of solving while alive.

After the burial the widow made up her mind to go to Mexico in person to handle the intricacies of her late husband's estate. In due course she arrived in Mexico City and almost at once made the acquaintance of a Madame Laforce who lived in a large home along the ultra-smart Avenue de los Caballeros. As a new arrival from a Paris literary set the novelist and poetess was very welcome among the group of friends encouraged and entertained by Madame Laforce. The group had a truly international complexion, and it was at such a gathering that Paul Jacques' handsome widow met for the first time a dark-faced man with sad brown eyes who smiled easily. He said his name was Weissmann, but as though to endorse the Rumanian origin he claimed he had adopted the Balkan-sounding name of Bessarabo.

He has been described as a mystery man. He was certainly accepted for what he purported to be, a European engaged in a world-wide timber trade, but he rarely referred to any activity that could be remotely connected with timber. He had money always available, his bank credit was good, and he had a good deal of time on his hands.

Madame Jacques found him attractive, her daughter of eleven years did not. Bessarabo was not discouraged by the unconcealed dislike of another man's offspring, and he continued paying court to that man's widow. Madame Jacques could not truthfully be said to have allowed herself to be swept off her feet. She was far too well adjusted and far-seeing. But she encouraged the Rumanian's suit, and presumably because her calculating mind had decided such a marriage would be to her advantage she agreed to change her status and name to that of Madame Bessarabo.

This was done in December.

Whereupon she decided the literary circles in Paris were again in need of her patronage and shining example. Accordingly the family arrived in the French capital and installed themselves in a fashionable apartment. Hera Bessarabo lost little time in preparing once more to pick up the threads of her past life of indulgence and shallow flattery.

However, there was something more than a short interval of time that marked a difference between the salon lioness that had been and the one that sought to be. Hera Bessarabo, ever on the *qui vive* for fresh sensation and a vicarious thrill, had succumbed to the enchantment of hashish and the potent promises of a drug made from Mexican mescal. She was fast becoming a drug addict, and this did not improve a temper that had been noted hitherto for its volatile quality.

The Bessarabo household became a storm centre, and the storms blew up with equatorial intensity and frequency. The man who had once been known as Weissmann learned the lesson that had brought sharp disillusion to Paul Jacques. It was on balance better to give way to his wife than oppose her wishes. On those occasions, when some flickering spark of masculine dignity demanded that he stand up to her tantrums, it was to hear her scream a disturbing phrase:

'I'll have your skin!'

It has been said she used the threat repeatedly when thwarted by Paule's stepfather. What she meant by the phrase has never been clear. What it came to mean in the long run is all too horribly clear, as it had been to Jacques, who was comfortably out of such domestic disturbances, and whose ghost, had it a mind to return to old haunts, might have viewed with ironic appreciation the marital martyrdom of a man who professed to know a great deal about timber, but allowed his wife to treat him as though he were a wormy log.

Madame Bessarabo might have been under the influence of hashish when she first tried to administer physical punishment to her husband. He awoke one night to find she had her hands around his throat and was pressing with a passion not dictated by love. When he overcame her apparent determination to return to the veiled state of widowhood she burst into tears and pleaded that she was overwrought.

The next time such a rage produced a similar state of mind she did not rely on her bare hands. She pointed a pistol at his head and shouted in Mexican Spanish, 'Out of my way or I'll remove you.' It was no idle boast. Almost before she had finished uttering the shouted words she was squeezing the trigger. Bessarabo had flung himself to the floor, thoroughly scared, and he had every right to be. The bullet whistled through the space he had been occupying seconds before.

Fire-arms were no innovation in his wife's life. Apart from the shooting that removed Paul Jacques permanently, there had been another violent episode in Mexico before she and Bessarabo had arrived at terms of intimacy. On that occasion also lead had sped from a gun. The real truth of the incident was about as well concealed as what had really happened to her first husband. What was known was that she and her small daughter had gone to the home of a wealthy Mexican ranchero in the countryside. The Mexican had died of gun wounds, and his distressed visitor had told the story of four horsemen arriving and shooting her friend before riding off again. The way the story was told it sounded like a vengeance plot. For the second time the police had accepted her version of a fatal incident because no other was offered.

But the sudden strikers of vengeance was a theme she was to resort to later, thousands of miles distant from the Mexican rancho. Bessarabo had a friend named Berlioz. One day he confided to this friend that he thought his wife would eventually treat him as she had the others, and left Berlioz to make what he would of the remark.

It was in February 1920 that she next got her hands clutched convulsively around his throat. Again her husband's masculine strength kept some air in his lungs. He decided it was high time to leave this woman whose fits of rage were apparently growing more and more uncontrollable. Moreover, the daughter had grown up resembling her mother, in looks, in temperament, in all those unprepossessing qualities that her mother reserved for her life behind the closed doors of their home. But there was no chance of Bessarabo getting off the domestic hook.

'Walk out on me,' his literary wife told him, 'and I'll go to the police. I'll expose you.'

The precise implication was never made clear, but it seemed to refer darkly to the manner in which the husband came by his wealth, so it can be assumed that the remark's origins were rooted in those first days in Mexico, when a man infatuated by a sophisticated Parisienne told her too many secrets when trying to impress her with his ability to keep her in that station to which she aspired.

Bessarabo remained on the hook. Uncomfortably on it.

Being a man capable of compromise and accommodation by temperament, he sought to ameliorate his harsh lot by the unpublicized purchase of a property at Montmorency, where from time to time he found relaxation and retreat in the company of other women. One of this very close circle was his secretary, to whom he imparted the fear that his wife and stepdaughter might have a design for murdering him. His secretary didn't seem alarmed. She probably knew her boss and his kind of tales, told when the level in the cognac bottle was sinking.

Bearing that in mind, it is curious that to another of the Montmorency mesdemoiselles he said that he might die if an enemy from his past found him.

There were occasions when he couldn't have been highly diverting as the great lover. Opportunity became appreciably less when Hera Bessarabo's keen nose ferreted out the love-nest. But the secretary stayed around as an accommodating wench on her day off. Bessarabo even revealed a capacity for growing fond of her in his fashion.

A month after the latest hands-round-his-neck bid Hera Bessarabo received a letter postmarked Mexico City. The concierge took it up to her, saw the letter opened and read, and then was surprised to see the hitherto self-contained and domineering Madame Bessarabo collapse and showing signs of fear. The concierge picked up the letter, glanced at the writing, but couldn't read a word of Spanish. That evening he heard a violent and loud quarrel in the Bessarabo apartment. It was more prolonged than usual.

For three days after that Bessarabo did not leave the apartment. When he stirred abroad he went in a hired car. At night he was particularly careful to lock all their doors and windows. According to the concierge he behaved like man overcome by fear.

It took a few weeks for him to pluck up the nerve to whip his secretary off for a brief stay at the Montmorency villa. The change wrought an improvement in his condition. When he returned to Paris he was even able to joke with the concierge, who wondered much, especially as that morning another letter bearing a Mexico City postmark had arrived, and Madame Bessarabo had reacted very much as before when she scanned the news in Spanish.

There followed another protracted quarrel. The concierge, now really agog with curiosity, stole up the stairs to eavesdrop, but was disappointed to hear Madame and Monsieur Bessarabo apparently slanging each other in a language that was foreign, but which he took to be Spanish.

That night the lights in the Bessarabo apartment remained burning until dawn. But bright and early Madame Bessarabo was up and about, and a short while later she told the concierge she and her daughter were going to the country, and that she wanted him to carry down their trunk and then to call a taxi.

The concierge had to be helped in handling the large trunk he found awaiting him in their apartment by the mother and daughter. Even so the trunk was bumped down most of the curving flight of stone stairs to street level. The concierge went to collect a taxi and when he returned with one the Bessarabo females were waiting with two valises. They, their valises, and the trunk were loaded into the taxi, which drove away.

But that evening the two women returned on foot. They were not exactly confiding, but apparently there had been a change of plans, and they were no longer willing to sojourn in the country.

In the following days Monsieur Bessarabo was not seen entering or leaving his apartment. A few friends were informed that he was away on business.

'I don't like it,' the hired-car driver told the concierge. He was a man given to much frowning, and he did not like women. They were poor tippers, he had found.

His name was Croix, and he looked it, a man who when crossed became belligerent, as he now was, and he thought with reason. Croix had driven Bessarabo around Paris for weeks and had been told never to be late when ordered. Bessarabo's tips had been generous, and Croix had become accustomed to this client—he did not want to lose him. On July 30th he had deposited Bessarabo at the door of the apartment building and had been given instructions to call in the morning at nine.

He had arrived, waited, and then sought the concierge to learn that the family was out, the womenfolk off to the country. When they had returned Croix came calling and was informed that Bessarabo was out of Paris.

After a few days he again made inquiries of the concierge.

'He's not back. No sign of him,' said the man.

'I still don't like it,' growled Croix darkly.

'But what can one do?'

'I could go to the police.'

The concierge made a sound that was not polite. But then the police was a subject most concierges were not prepared to be polite about. They fought a never-ending fight over local regulations supported by pin-pricking police action. However, Croix felt put out at losing his tips, and he was quite prepared to make trouble for someone to relieve his feelings, so he called at the police station in the Quartier Saint-Georges and delivered himself of the opinion that something was curious about Monsieur Bessarabo of the Square Bruyère.

With the complaint on record, the local detectives went round to have some words with the concierge. They shed their former lassitude when they heard of the big and very heavy trunk. Such pieces of luggage are invariably suspect in inquiries where someone is missing after known quarrels. Moreover, the picture of life in the Bessarabo apartment as offered by the concierge was not one of domestic harmony. They tried to trace the trunk and started by locating the taxi driver, which wasn't too difficult, only to learn from him that the trunk and his female passengers had been taken to the Gare du Nord, where they had disembarked and he had left them.

The detectives tried to find a porter who had collected the big trunk. They drew blank.

They went back to No. 3 Square Bruyère to start again, this time by interviewing Madame Bessarabo. She had a tailored story to offer. It was true her husband had returned late at night as Croix had said, but he had spent most of his time in the apartment packing the large trunk. He had left the apartment early in the morning after telling her to meet him with the trunk at eleven o'clock at the Gare du Nord in time to catch a train for Montmorency. She remembered seeing him collect a large number of papers and documents from a drawer which he had always kept locked.

'Why are you taking those?' she had asked.

'I want to destroy them after reading them through,' he had said without enlarging.

She had arrived at the Gare du Nord with her daughter and the trunk at about ten-thirty. She wanted to be in good time. But her husband had not put in an appearance, and she had thought that he had gone off with his secretary. She had taken her daughter to the Gare de Lyon, across the river, had lunch in the station restaurant, then returned to the Gare du Nord, where Bessarabo was pacing up and down. He told her his plans had changed. He had the trunk brought from where she had deposited it, put it in a taxi, and drove off with it after telling her he would be coming back.

She had waited for an hour, which was just as well if her story had any truth, for the taxi driver who had collected her husband now returned with the trunk still in his cab. Her husband wanted her to send the trunk on to Nancy, the taxi driver said. So she had got into the cab and been driven to the Gare de l'Est, where she had put the trunk on an eastbound train and taken a third-class ticket to Nancy, which is the capital of Lorraine.

She had neither seen nor heard from her husband since that afternoon.

'I think,' she finished her story, 'he's gone off with his secretary, possibly to Rumania, where he was born.'

The story was full of false touches, but this last was well-nigh more than the hard-grained Paris cops could take without letting her see they thought she was a rare liar. But they trailed off to the Gare de l'Est, and sure enough such a large trunk had been sent on to Nancy. A form with the name Bessarabo on it was dug out of the receipt files. A clerk recalled the young woman who signed the form. She answered to the description of Paule Jacques, whose name had never been changed to her stepfather's.

The detectives then discovered, after making inquiries in the shopping area the mother and daughter patronized, that she had bought several metres of rubberized sheeting as well as a length of manilla rope on August 1st. The following day Madame Bessarabo had presented to a notary what she claimed was a power of attorney, duly signed by her husband, authorizing her to be paid more than half a million francs which was due on July 31st to Bessarabo on commission on a very large oil deal.

The documents relating to the oil deal had been found among her husband's papers. They would have been valid if the deal had gone through, but it hadn't.

When this was explained to her, and she understood she couldn't collect the money, she became abusive.

What the detectives had found out was told to the local *juge d'instruction*. He authorized them to go to Nancy, where the trunk, still being held at the station for collection, was found intact. It was speedily opened, and inside was a man's body dressed in a red flannel undergarment; he was in a sitting posture, held in that position by a stout leather strap. It was impossible to say who the man was for his face had been beaten to a mask of pulp. Every feature had been destroyed. There was a bullet hole in the back of the terrible head. The trunk which had been used as a portable coffin had been lined with rubberized sheeting.

Some hours later the corpse without a face, removed from its red flannel shroud, lay in a Paris morgue, and Madame Bessarabo was asked to take a look at it.

'This cannot be the body of my husband,' she said very readily. 'Monsieur Bessarabo was slimmer and younger in every way. This is the body of a fat man.'

She was pressed for a more detailed statement, and this time she said the letters from Mexico City had originated from members of a secret society who had decided her husband must die. Her husband had become frightened, and cleared out all the papers he had concerning the activities of this secret society to which he had belonged. This was the only addition to her previous very thin tale.

The shades of those four horsemen at the rancho were on the move. However, as a variant, it was not an improvement on the previous story that had satisfied the Mexican police. The Paris police had heard fanciful tales before. But their job was to establish proof or lack of it, so they tracked down Mademoiselle Nollet, the very obliging secretary, only to be told she knew nothing and to hear her repeat it every time they tried a fresh question.

They found a boat attendant at Enghien who had rented a rowing boat to a couple of women who might have been Hera Bessarabo and her daughter. The women had taken two objects out in the boat, which might have been valises, but when they returned the boat was empty. The younger said her companion had been sick, but that could not account for the large quantity of water in the bottom of the boat, as though it had been shipped when the boat tipped as one or both had leaned over one side with something weighted.

Because the boatman thought the younger woman looked like Paule Jacques the lake was dragged. The dragging proved to be a waste of time. Back to Paris went detectives who were beginning to feel frustrated, and to think with good reason they had been led a wild-goose chase.

Madame Bessarabo received another call from them. The detectives were armed with fresh questions that required new answers. She hedged and said cannily that if the dead man could possibly be her husband, then the person responsible for his murder was a Señor Becker, an enemy of her husband in South America.

Now occurred one of those coincidences that happen outrageously in real life, as records prove, but to which no fiction writer dare aspire. A man named Becker committed suicide in the Bois de Boulogne a short while after Madame Bessarabo offered her latest titbit to the police. They worked desperately to link the dead Becker with the dead Bessarabo, but could prove no connection.

Belatedly perhaps the two women were arrested and lodged in the prison of Saint-Lazare. The elder, isolated for the first time, took the occasion to divest herself of a new statement. But like all her statements she made it into quite a production.

She said that a letter from her husband's secretary had fallen from Bessarabo's pocket on the evening of July 30th, and when they quarrelled about it he struck her. 'Brutally' was the word she used to the police. She had then snatched up a gun to scare him into leaving her alone. But it had gone off in their joint excitement, and he had been wounded fatally.

The police remained sceptical; her stories showed no sign of improving.

She had continued with the statement, and had then explained how she had consequently told her daughter, when the girl was roused by the shot, to go away. She said Paule had nothing to do with the tragedy and was not even present when the shot was fired, but had come into the room later to inquire what the shot meant.

She had soon found out.

But her mother insisted that her daughter had been told to go away. It was she, Hera, having sufficiently recovered, who had later packed the corpse in the trunk and dispatched it to Nancy. All the girl had done was help her to get the trunk down from where it was stored on the sixth floor with other pieces of luggage and empty packages.

However, this statement at any rate provided the police with an admission of shooting Bessarabo. They now had to return to checking out the statements and the evidence. But they came upon another piece of negative evidence, which was far from encouraging. When the taxi driver who had picked up the trunk at the Gare du Nord was eventually traced and found, after a considerable search, he failed to recognize either of the two women arrested.

Meantime Paris was in a fever of excitement about the case with lengthy columns appearing daily in the popular organs of the Press, and dramatic announcements expected to keep interest growing, at least until the trial, which opened at the Seine Assize Court on the 15th of February, 1921. It soon became a wrangling match between histrionic advocates who were aware of strutting their stage in a drenching limelight. The arguments went to and fro between counsel and defendants, interpersed with passionate avowals and declarations on the part of the mother. The fury eventually ground to a halt, and when at last the final piece of an incredible drama of mystery which kept the Paris audience agog was wrung from the conflicting and confusing evidence, Paule Jacques sprang a surprise, quite unexpected, which brought the case to shuddering life again.

She suddenly called to the court, 'The truth! I have to proclaim the truth!'

After her words there was a pregnant silence save for a moan from her mother, who fainted. The Bench ordered the young woman to unburden herself of the truth without further delay. Whereupon she began another incredible story. Her stepfather had been a brute. No woman had been safe from his lust, and many times he had tried to seduce her. Her mother lived in terror of his rages and animalism. She told how she had run into the living-room after hearing the shot.

'Oh, God!' she exclaimed. 'What have you done, Mother?'

'Go back to bed,' Madame Bessarabo had ordered, adding, 'What has happened is only justice.'

She had tried to argue with her mother, and remembered her saying, 'It was his life or mine. Now go to bed and leave me.'

She wanted to call the police, she said, but her mother would not allow this. She had seen the face of a figure covered by a sheet with spreading bloodstains. Her mother dragged her away, saying, 'You must never know who it is. But it is not your stepfather. I can't tell you the awful secret of what happened tonight.'

The young woman in the dock had got this far when her mother recovered and sat up, crying, '*Calle te!*' The sudden use of a Spanish command to be silent made Paule break down. There was uproar as the girl continued with her story of how that night and for the next few days her mother had kept her locked in her room until she was forced to type at dictation speed a formularized power of attorney.

'Sign his name—Bessarabo,' she was ordered.

The taking of the roped trunk was given a new version. The only point they had in common was the destination—Nancy. Then Paule ended her interrupted outburst with the words, 'That is the complete truth.' Some minutes later her mother was asked if she had anything to say. But Madame Bessarabo had sunk into herself. She shook her head and muttered, 'I have nothing to say except my daughter did what she did because I told her. You must acquit her.'

The muddled and untidy case was left for the jury, who decided on a verdict of guilty with extenuating circumstances, which meant that the daughter would be freed.

As the cynical were quick to observe, Paule had bought her freedom by shopping her mother, who was duly sentenced to penal servitude for twenty years. She received the sentence with almost contemptuous composure. The young woman stared at her in horror and promptly became shriekingly hysterical.

5

ENGLAND

What Happened to Muriel McKay?

Detective Chief Superintendent Wilfred Smith had reluctantly come to the decision that Mrs Muriel McKay had vanished. Early in the New Year of 1970 he was sure of it, the feeling of certainty was in his bones.

She had disappeared from her husband's home in Arthur Road, Wimbledon, a thoroughfare of good-class substantial houses with neatly arranged flower-beds and trim hedges and lawns not far from a busy artery in south-west London. As the days continued without news of her the police intensified their hunt for clues that might provide an answer to the mystery, which was to result in Britain's first adult kidnapping, followed by murder and a possible solution to a truly horrendous crime.

It all began when Alick McKay arrived home one December night shortly before eight o'clock and found the house in darkness and his wife absent.

'Are you in, Muriel?' he called.

There was no reply. He stooped to pick up several pieces of newspaper by the front door and tossed them into the garden, where they would have been caught by a wintry gust of wind. He rang the door-bell, but had to use his key. When he switched the light on he saw that a chair had been pulled into the middle of the hall and there were sheets of newspaper on the normally tidy floor. He turned and saw that the telephone was off the hook, with the number disc missing, as though it had been flung down in a hurry. Some wire twine lay on a chair, and on the writing-table for notes was a billhook. At the sight of this last item Alick McKay suddenly felt the first twinges of alarm. He hurried through the rooms in the empty house, calling to his wife. He ran out to the garden, and found his wife's car parked in the garage next to his own.

More slowly he went back into the house; it seemed that someone had forced the door, and a wide strip of sticking plaster had been dropped, with the adhesive side smudged as though it had been restuck. By now he was feeling more than mere twinges of alarm. He dashed across the road to the house of a neighbour.

'I must 'phone the police,' he said excitedly. 'Something seems to have happened to Muriel.'

Very soon CID detectives appeared in Arthur Road, and they learned that Alick McKay, a man of sixty, was the acting chairman of the *News of the World* Organization, and after taking a statement they were passed on to Wilfred Smith, a senior detective at Scotland Yard, who was put in charge of the case by the Assistant Commissioner when large headlines announced that there was a mystery right on Fleet Street's own doorstep.

Telephones in the McKay household were ordered to be tapped, a direction given only in exceptional circumstances. As soon as the news was received that Mrs McKay had vanished from Wimbledon, reporters covered the house and Arthur Road on a dark cold night without expecting any real news. But in the event their vigil was not wasted. It was late at night when a disguised voice rang the missing woman's home. The man who made the call claimed extravagantly, 'I am speaking from Mafia Group Three.' He then paused to add, 'From America.'

A hoax? Anything was possible at this stage. A police spokesman nodded to the *News of the World* executive, who asked the disguised voice what he wanted to get his wife returned safely.

'One million pounds by Wednesday night,' was the grim ultimatum.

Muriel McKay had disappeared on December 29th. The kidnapper had sounded in a hurry as he informed whoever was listening that if the money was not paid Mrs McKay would die. Then the 'phone went dead. However, he put through another call over the public line, as though he had had an afterthought.

'Your wife has written a letter to you,' he said. 'Read it carefully.'

Again he rang off, leaving a dialling tone to burr in a shocked husband's ear as a police officer replaced the instrument.

Time passed on dragging feet as Alick McKay waited for the arrival of the letter from his wife. The promised letter duly came on the last day of the year, and McKay was convinced that it was not a cruel hoax perpetrated by an unfeeling mischief-maker. The letter ran:

'Alick darling, I am blindfolded and cold. Only blankets. Please do something to get me home. I think of you constantly, and the family and friends. I have been calm so far, darling. What have I done to deserve this treatment? Can you do something please, soon?'

The police experts digested the terms of the letter, but there were some sceptics who felt that the affair might be a strange kind of publicity stunt engendered by the husband. The host of theories varied from the story of a secret bag of jewellery that had disappeared in the wife's custody, to the impossibility of arranging a ransom as the price for such an abduction. But even the notion of a British-inspired kidnapping was one that was repugnant to the average man in the street, and he was bewildered by the reports of both police and journalists.

'The whole thing is too fantastic,' summed up one body of opinion. 'Kidnappers can't get away with anything like this in Britain.'

It took Alick McKay to disillusion them as unbelievers and the mystery of what happened to his wife Muriel to convince them that it not only could, but had. Many had to stop believing in a sort of Cloud Cuckoo Land—the ugly and the frightening had become the everyday.

In the dramatic interim the husband told the Press, 'I am

appalled by the suggestions that signs of intruders found after my wife vanished were planted. There is no basis whatsoever for such insinuations. The whole thing has had a most unhappy effect on myself and my family. We are most concerned for my wife's safety and we have no doubt that my wife is being held somewhere.'

In support of denial of rumours and extravagant theories Scotland Yard issued a direct statement.

'Following reports in the Press,' said the statement, 'the police wish to confirm that the disappearance of Mrs McKay is being taken seriously as a case of abduction.'

Meantime Chief Superintendent Wilfred Smith and his able assistant Detective Inspector John Minors of the Wimbledon CID were covering such leads as remained open for reasonable investigation without infringing the rights of a worried and at times near-demented husband who was becoming daily more anxious for his wife's safety. One thing was certain. Should a private ransom be paid to the kidnapper or kidnappers there was no way of ensuring that Muriel McKay would be returned safe and without harm or injury. This was what nagged at the mind of Alick McKay.

For there were a good many hoax callers who purported to be able to help find his wife, and these had to be separated from the helpful intentions of genuine inquiries, like chaff from grain. The number of police working on the case grew; they eventually included men from the Flying Squad, others from the No. 9 Regional Crime Squad, and again more from the Special Patrol Group. In all some five thousand officers and men came to be involved in the investigation. But the time was wearing for the husband, who watched day succeed day with no confirmed news.

On January 9th he made the effort to give a television appearance in which he appealed to the men responsible for the kidnapping to send him something personal that belonged to his wife and might prove that she was still alive. The response was speedy. By post the next day came items of clothing that Alick McKay could readily recognize. But pieces of clothing were not in themselves proof that Muriel McKay was still alive, and the police had to be extremely cautious in not lifting McKay's hopes too high. For now nearly a fortnight had elapsed since the call said to have been made by the Mafia and the demand for a million in ransom money.

On the other hand, some quite unscrupulous characters had tried their hands at fraud and blackmail, and several arrests resulted when they were traced.

Indeed Diane McKay, Muriel's daughter, who had been told to take a bus to a certain rendezvous and leave a sum of money, was impersonated by a sergeant named White. But a sharp-eyed bus conductress had glimpsed White's hairy leg and immediately became suspicious. He was stopped by a couple of uniformed constables and held until explanations were forthcoming. Such tragicomic incidents were fortunately not frequent, but they underlined the lengths to which the police went and the pains taken by them to achieve anything that could be seen as a valid result of the efforts being made in the glare of unrelenting publicity. Such an operation was new to the men making it, and they were perhaps anxious not to commit errors that might be irretrievable.

On one occasion, desperate for real news to break his wife's continued silence, the husband and his family made contact with a Dutch clairvoyant, who journeyed to England to interview the newspaper executive. But although Gerard Croiset said he could see that two coloured men were involved in the kidnapping, and could also see a farmhouse, and that the route from Wimbledon had led to Epping, north of London, he was not able to pinpoint the locality more closely, and the excursion into the supernatural faded, while the host of rumours increased and circulated.

Perhaps because of McKay's dogged insistence, several contacts with the believed kidnappers were made while the winter weeks were wearing away. Because of his pugnacious refusal to let-up he received another letter from 'M3'. In this his son Ian was instructed to go to a call box in Edmonton with a ransom of half a million in a black suitcase. Seemingly the kidnappers, with the police so wary and active, were ready to cut the agreed price by fifty per cent.

This time Sergeant Roger Street impersonated the son. This attempt to hand over the ransom failed. Possibly because the police felt they could not afford to take more than what seemed to them a reasonable risk. In yet another Ian McKay told the kidnappers that he had injured an arm, and could not drive. This was a subterfuge to enable Sergeant Street to hide a walkie-talkie in a sling while Inspector Minors posed as the chauffeur driving a Rolls owned by the *News of the World*. A package of fake notes was made to look like hundreds of pounds of real cash. Yard detectives followed at discreet intervals.

The Rolls arrived in Edmonton, and the bogus son was instructed by 'phone: 'Proceed along the Cambridge Road away from London. At the second set of traffic lights on the left is Southbury Road, with a telephone box at the corner. Go there and wait for me. Any error will be fatal.'

They drove to the next rendezvous at ten forty-five. The telephone rang and Street, speaking as Ian, answered. He was told to look at the floor, where a cigarette packet containing instructions had been placed. Ian was told to continue to Dane End, where he would see two paper flowers on a bank by the roadside. That was where he was to leave the money and then return to the first call box, where he would receive yet another call informing him where his mother was. The Rolls arrived at Dane End, saw the paper flowers, and placed the money on the verge. They then returned to the first call box, while at the scene of the ransom pick-up the police waited. But there were so many police cars and disguised officers that the kidnappers had no trouble in spotting the roadside trap. Later, after the pick-up had been called off, one of them told Ian McKay from Arthur Road, 'There were at least twenty cars. Four motor-bikes. Saw lots of white helmets,' he said in a clipped voice in short phrases. 'I saw you when you went there, I saw you. I saw you, you know,' and after some more rambling, he added in a tone of complaint, 'I took your word for granted, believed you, trusted you.'

By this time the police were getting a clearer picture of the kidnappers. With his intonation one could be an Indian or a Pakistani, while the search had been narrowed to Essex. But that still left a great deal of territory for the police to comb through.

In the meantime, what had happened to Muriel McKay? That remained a key question that could not be answered.

But at the back of their minds certain members of the police had a growing fear. Was she still alive?

The police renewed their intentions to make a deal if it was possible. On February 5th a new and elaborate runaround was started hopefully. Minors, posing as Alick McKay, with a female detective, Constable Joyce Armitage, dressed as Muriel McKay's daughter, drove to Bethnal Green in the now familiar Rolls with two suitcases of fake money. In the Rolls' boot a police marksman was concealed, Inspector Bland. Again a worn routine was followed. A 'phone rang in a public call box and when the instrument was lifted they were told to take the Underground to Epping Station. There they received another 'phone call. This time they were to go by rail to Bishop's Stortford, then take a taxi to a place where the money was to be left. Bland, who had not had a very comfortable journey, followed the routine to the letter, and managed to get into a hedge just before the two cases were set in position. Screened by the evergreen hedge, he watched a Volvo drive up. It stopped beside the suitcases, but drove on when a car behind could not pass in the narrow lane. The patient Bland waited, and half an hour later saw the same Volvo return. As it slowed another car braked just in front of them. A man and woman climbed out. They looked at the suitcases, obviously discussing what should be done with them. The man then got back into the car and returned a few minutes later with a local policeman, who took charge of the cases.

Again the best-laid schemes of mice and police had been frustrated.

However, the police had taken a note of the Volvo's number.

It was registered in the name of Arthur Hosein, who occupied Rook's Farm, Stocking Pelham, in Hertfordshire. Two days later after making cautious local inquiries there was a sudden descent by armed police on the farm. Arthur Hosein and his younger brother Nizamodeen looked on as the police began a thorough search. The brothers were Indian immigrants from Trinidad. When addressed they remained dumb, and the younger seemed scared.

It didn't take the police long to make sure that Muriel McKay was not being held prisoner anywhere on the farm. Dogs were employed in a close search, and then special Commando police, before a full body of more than two hundred police searchers, who spent two weeks covering the ground inch by inch, only to draw blank, and finally to call a halt. Muriel McKay had not been found.

But in those two weeks there had been a great deal of activity while the Press continued to announce startling developments that were eagerly anticipated. An RAF helicopter had photographed the farm and the ground around it. Wells and ponds were emptied. Forensic workers checked metal scrapings, bonfire ash, and all chemicals, and they even dusted for scraps of Muriel McKay's fingerprints, but no recognizable impressions were found. The actual farmhouse was taken apart in a gruesome search for bones and splintered particles. None was found.

But other significant clues were found, such as paper flowers similar to those left at the ransom rendezvous, coloured writing paper of the quality and kind used by Muriel McKay to pen letters to her husband; and a palm-print, taken from a piece of newsprint at the home in Arthur Road, matched one of the palms of Nizamodeen Hosein.

The circuitous route to a solution of the mystery was at last completed after a great deal of work and the expending of many futile man-hours. The Hosein brothers were duly arrested and charged with murder. Their inimical stares remained blank and their mouths remained shut, clamped tight.

It took five months for the police to complete all the remaining work that had to be done before the accused could be brought to trial. By this time there was a world-wide interest in the mystery. A great many details had to be confirmed, and an incredible story evolved as the framework of the case against the accused took filled-in shape. But at last, by September 24th, Mr Justice Sebag Shaw was ready to open the proceedings at the Old Bailey, and Alick McKay, looking somewhat drawn and tense, faced the dark-skinned pair in the dock whose silence, he believed, held the key to what had happened to his wife. His evidence told of the discovery of his wife's absence and gave details of the ensuing weeks without news of her. When he left the witness box he did not glance at the defendants.

The prosecution got down to detailed aspects of the investigation, and Chief Inspector Arthur Brine related the quest for fingerprints. Apart from the palm-print, he had found various prints belonging to the elder brother of the pair in the dock, and he told the court, 'The most important factors in fingerprinting are the ridge characteristics left in the impressions. I would be satisfied with eight, but we found sixteen, which puts it beyond all reasonable doubt in my opinion.'

Griffith Davis, an actor, told the court of meeting Arthur Hosein in the Raven public-house at Berden, in Essex. He had met Hosein previously and in a talk with him had heard how his father was an *imam*, or Mohammedan priest, living in Trinidad. On the 6th of February when Hosein appeared at the Raven he was drinking double whiskies and told Davis how he planned to become a millionaire like his father. However, the truth was explained by Sir Peter Rawlinson, the Attorney-General, leading for the Crown. The father was not a millionaire, as the son had boasted in the Raven, but he was a highly respected member of the Trinidad community, who was intending to visit his sons in Britain, and it was possible that he had heard of the elder son's imaginary riches, resulting in the intention to pay a visit. This would expose the falsity of the bogus claims. The sons therefore concocted a scheme for getting rich quick.

The scheme was given shape when, in a television interview with Rupert Murdoch, chairman of the *News of the World* Organization, David Frost mentioned the fact that his guest was a millionaire. That was on October 9th. Almost at once the Hosein brothers started to plan a kidnapping for ransom. They watched Mr Murdoch's Rolls and made the mistake of confusing the Murdoch's house in Arthur Road with the McKay home. They found out their mistake when in December 1969, a week before Christmas, Mr and Mrs Murdoch left England for Australia. Alick McKay was left in charge of the newspaper.

The upshot was that in their minds they had confused the Murdochs with the McKays. Instead of kidnapping Mrs Murdoch, now safely in Australia, they had grabbed Muriel McKay—the wrong victim.

However, once the crime had been committed there seemed no way the mistake could be rectified except by brazening it out, and that was where the personality of the brothers came into forceful consideration, for there was no question that the elder of the pair was the more dominant individual and capable of overriding the younger's objections and fears. Consequently, the high spots of the trial were achieved when Arthur Hosein, the first witness for the defence, went into the witness box and began to tell his story with his defence counsel, Mr Barry Hudson, QC, listening to his performance and watching it closely.

Hosein was thirty-four, twelve years older than his brother. He had a fashion-plate appearance, being dressed in a mohair suit of black with a cut-away coat, white shirt, and black bow-tie. As one reporter remarked, 'He looked as though he wanted to cut a dash.' He described himself as a fashion designer who owned a house in Stocking Pelham. There he lived with his wife and three children. His brother had come to live with them about four months before Christmas. Two months before his wife had taken the children on a trip to Germany, where she was born. He claimed that on the 29th of December, while he was still suffering from a bad chest, he had said goodnight to his brother about half-past seven and went to bed, taking a bottle of Scotch and some ginger ale with him.

'About two am, he said, 'I went downstairs and found my brother with four men. I think one was British, one American, and the other two, one looked like Maurice Chevalier, I think were Frenchmen. The 'phone rang twice. The first time I let Nizam answer it. The second time it was a girl friend for my brother. I didn't know where he was.'

At this point his denial ran into difficulties, and when reference was made to a call received by the McKays he began gesticulating with his hands and his words became uncertain and stopped. At this Mr Justice Shaw spoke to him.

'Please try to keep your hands down,' he cautioned. 'All your gesticulating is distracting the jury.'

He dropped his hands, attempted to square his shoulders, and went on: 'I was drinking heavily. I heard voices. I thought my brother had left the television on. I sleep in my shorts and, not expecting anyone to be there, I went downstairs. But there were some men with my brother. My brother said to me that these men had influence in the House of Commons. They were about to try to get him a permanent stay in this country. It sounds in this court as if it were fiction. But my brother's ignorance of the fact that he has been used to reciprocate help they were offering him to stay on in this country, he was persuaded to do such things as cruise around some arid zone where there was one million pounds.'

The public in the Old Bailey court stirred restively at this. It was the first mention of a million pounds.

The witness went on not very coherently, 'They offered me a drink of my own whisky. I had one drink and went to bed. This incident was before Christmas. I saw these men on two occasions in my lounge.'

Patently it seemed that the defendant was having some trouble with remembering the occasion to which he referred, and his concentration appeared to be wavering. Instead of clearing a hurdle, he had collided with it, and only extracted himself with further hazards.

The defence counsel elicited the information that February 1st was the date when the ransom money was alleged to have been left near the paper flowers. On that day the brothers went to London with a tailor, according to the elder, but they had separated. After hearing the ten o'clock news he went to bed and his brother returned home later.

'His clothes were very wet,' said the defendant, 'and I did not intend to ask him where he had been as he was in a very bad way. He told me the next day he had 'phoned his girl friend, and I presume she had not been in, and he had hitch-hiked home.'

But presumptions were not quite good enough for a jury patiently waiting to learn what had happened to the missing Muriel McKay. Also mere repetition of alleged facts and allegations was not serving their arrival at a conclusion. There were too many scraps of asides. However, the charged man got the bit between his teeth when he claimed that the police in Wimbledon, after he had been arrested at the farm and driven to South London, had subjected him to a form of what he referred to as mental torture.

'I was tortured mentally and physically by the police when they interrogated me. I have co-operated in every way with the police. But I was very badly treated by them. Smith beat hell out of me while under the influence of drink. He had a bottle of Scotch in front of him. He hit my belly and slapped my face. I also starved for two nights and had not slept for two nights. I was awakened by police every ten minutes.'

He saw the jury looking at him with stone faces.

'As for the statement the police say I made,' he hurried on with trembling and mobile hands, 'these are the police's own words. A statement made to implicate me of this terrible crime. This vindictiveness, this wickedness, this cruelty of the police, is hard to believe.' He turned to the judge and said with emphasis,

'My Lord is not aware of such things.'

He denied that he had written any ransom note, and ended with a touch of rhetoric that was apparently wasted.

'If you will believe what my brother will say about me, find me guilty on all charges,' he told the jury. 'I have lost my prestige and my character. Now I am fighting for my sanity. I am innocent of all charges.'

It was an inflated performance, but the jury did not appear to be ready to take up any challenge he had had laid down.

Then it was the younger brother's turn to face his counsel, Mr Douglas Draycott. After admitting that he was not always on the best of terms with his brother, who asked him to help around the farm and sometimes gave him pocket money when he ran errands for him, Nizam Hosein agreed that he was trying to arrange a permanent residence in Britain and then said his brother had absolutely no reason to be afraid of him, which was a gratuitous assertion that could have given the jury pause. Especially as interruptions started to be levelled, sometimes pertinently.

'Did you tell Nizam to stick two paper flowers on the roadside bank near Dane End?' asked Mr Draycott, which Arthur Hosein heatedly denied. And again, 'Is it true that when Nizam asked why he had to pick up a suitcase by the road on February 1st you quarrelled and pushed Nizam out of the car?' Mr Draycott inquired.

'It's not true,' retorted Arthur Hosein.

'Is it not true that on February 6th you told Nizam to collect two suitcases at Bishop's Stortford?' came another bland question.

'Not true,' shouted the elder brother, but there was now a desperate air about him. 'I am not concerned with what Nizam will say. I am concerned with what I am saying here now.'

Then the exchange of cross-examination produced real bite.

'Can you tell the court,' asked Mr Draycott, 'how the newspapers got into the house in Arthur Road when Mrs McKay disappeared?'

There was a pregnant silence until the elder brother said, 'If I were to commit a crime, would I take a newspaper and leave it at anyone's place?'

The attentive Mr Justice Shaw interposed with some advice for the irate Hosein. He warned him not to scorn counsel.

But the exchanges warmed up when the Attorney-General cross-examined Arthur Hosein about dates and the paper flowers.

'Would that be true?' he asked bluntly.

'I would deny. It would be untrue,' said the man being driven into a tight corner.

And about the suitcases on February 6th, inquired Sir Peter, 'Would that be true or false?'

'It would be false.'

So a classic case of when rogues fall out developed much to the jury's edification. There was a great deal of further cross-examination by police witnesses and others, but the exposed details could no longer conceal the grisly truth of a terrible crime without a body.

In his eventual summing-up Sir Peter Rawlinson stated: 'Both of these accused have been saying, "Not me, not me. I did no crime, but he did." This is, you may think, a pointer to you that the very fact of this behaviour may help to satisfy you about the guilt of these men. You may wonder how you may be asked to treat this case as murder when a body has never been found. I wish to put it to you that there were such circumstances as rendered the commission of a crime certain. There can be no other rational explanation than that Mrs McKay died. You may think that Mrs McKay, trussed and gagged, was forced into the boot of the car and taken away. Was there ever any thought of releasing her? If she was to be released, would she not have been able to identify those taking her?'

After a dramatic pause the Attorney-General stopped asking questions and made an assertion.

'Mrs Muriel McKay,' he said pointedly, 'had her death warrant signed the moment she was kidnapped.'

However, it was Mr Draycott who revived interest of what had happened to the victim's body when he made his last plea in support of his young client. Referring to the brothers, he said, 'It does not follow because one is guilty both are.' He went on: 'Local rumour was in two other cases that the victim was fed to the pigs. There is a similar rumour around this case. But there was forensic evidence—no body—but forensic evidence.' He stressed the point. 'The point here is that there is no evidence of Mrs McKay being fed to the pigs. Although the probability is that Mrs McKay is dead, she may not have been murdered.' He added finally, 'How she met her death we don't know.'

But by then the jury had a pretty fair idea of the grim nature of what had happened at Rook's Farm. When they retired the Press were expecting they would take two days deliberating the case. Instead it took the jury a mere four hours to resolve all the points and questions of a very complex case of murder. They reached the conclusion after the fifteen days of trial and found both defendants guilty of murdering Muriel McKay, but added a single recommendation to the judge. They asked him to extend leniency towards the younger brother.

'Thank you, members of the jury,' shouted the elder. 'It is a grave injustice.'

The judge then sentenced them to life imprisonment, enumerating the lesser crimes. 'I am not at all sure,' said Mr Justice Shaw, addressing the younger, 'you are any degree less culpable or less evil, but the jury have taken the view that you were less culpable.'

A grim-faced Alick McKay left the court slowly, like a man in a daze.

6

CANADA

Passion that Passed for Love

'Can I help you?' inquired the pretty girl with a pleasing smile.

The man looked at her. He seemed hesitant and unsure of himself as he stopped at the airport counter. Then, under the girl's scrutiny, he seemed to make up his mind.

'I want to book a passage for my wife on tomorrow's flight,' he said.

'Of course, sir,' she said encouragingly, and then paused. She turned to a page in her flight book, and said, 'I'm sorry, sir. All flights are booked until the 9th, but it's just possible we might get a cancellation.' She peered at the page of figures and times and made a helpful suggestion. 'If you like I'll put your wife's name on a waiting list I have. Then she can be assured of a seat on the first available flight.'

The man nodded. Lucille Levesque worked at the ticket counter at Ancienne Lorette Airport, Quebec. As she reached for her passenger list for the next day, September 7th, 1949, she quickly scanned it and wrote down Rita Guay, the name the man had given her. As she looked up the man asked a question.

'Can you also tell me how I can take out insurance for the trip?' Again he hesitated, like a man not conversant with details and regulations. 'For instance, if something happens on the flight, who will be the beneficiary?'

The bright-eyed French-Canadian girl was used to similar questions from puzzled travellers.

'You of course, Mr Guay, as your wife's husband, naturally. Do you want to fill out an insurance form?'

The man's eyes dropped from the girl's inquiring face. His chin went up and down in a brusque nod.

'In that case I suppose I'd best take out a policy,' he conceded.

He felt for his money and paid the premium on a one-flight policy for insurance valued at ten thousand dollars. The policy was on the traveller's life and was not for the round trip, which would have included the return journey. Whoever Mr Guay was, he seemed to be careful with money. With the insurance policy stamped, and the receipt safe in his pocket, he thanked Lucille Levesque, accepted another of her smiles, and left the airport building. Later he had a 'phone call from her, for she had taken the customer's telephone number.

'I'm pleased to tell you, Mr Guay, that I've had a cancellation for tomorrow,' she said in her pleasant voice. 'I can now accommodate Mrs Guay after all.'

The reply she received was not pleasant, and it was certainly surprising.

'Too late,' snapped the man who had been anxious to book for the flight. 'We'll have to make it the day you originally suggested, September 9th.'

'Very well, Mr Guay,' said the booking clerk, still trying to sound pleasant. 'In that case I'll cancel the cancellation and let September 9th stand. Thank you, sir.'

She rang off and forgot the indecisive man at the airport who had originally booked too late for his wife's flight, while in her home Mrs Guay was packing in preparation for the local flight. Her husband seemingly had other matters to attend to, and it was not until early on the morning of the 9th that he called on a certain Mrs Petri. The couple eyed each other as will people who have been lovers and know what it means for passion and desire to wane like an unfed fire.

The woman couldn't resist a feminine taunt about the past.

'I haven't seen much of you since you fell for that young angel, Joseph,' she observed.

The man scowled. He had no wish to quarrel about Angel Mary. Besides, they had been all through that a good while ago, and each knew where the other stood. He came to the point, as was his way when he wanted something, for he was a selfish man and acquisitive.

'I want you to do something for me, Marie.'

'Any reason?' inquired Marie Petri archly.

'Reason enough. I can't do it myself.'

'What is it, Joseph?'

'I want you to take a parcel to the airport for me. I can't make time myself. It's a religious statuette.'

The glances of the pair clashed in a duel of understanding, and perhaps perception on the part of the woman.

'I'm too sick to go, Joseph,' she said, trying to make it a flat refusal.

But there was more than understanding in the man's grin. There was knowledge.

'You won't be, Marie, if I cancel those promissory notes of yours,' he said nastily. 'They're locked up in the bank, so you be well enough to take the parcel for me, and then you can forget about those notes.'

Marie Petri appeared to make a remarkable recovery from her alleged bout of sickness, for she knew that Joseph Guay held her indeed over a barrel, and she had no alternative but to do what he wanted.

'Very well, Joseph,' she agreed demurely, but there was thought and speculation in her eyes.

It was some time later when she summoned a taxi and told the driver, Paul Pelletier, to go to the airport as she had a parcel. He saw that it was packed for air freight as he put it down on the front seat. He drove to the airport, where his passenger, dressed soberly in black, plumpish and with a turned-up nose, paid off Pelletier and marched off with the package to the weighing counter for freight. The parcel was weighed, the description checked—'a religious statuette'—the freight cost was paid and receipted, and the package placed with other articles going out on that day's flight. The plump woman in black walked away from the weighing counter. She made her way home, still thoughtful.

Some time later Joseph Guay and his dark-complexioned wife Rita arrived at the airport. Mrs Guay hurried through the glass door to the booking clerk, and received one of Lucille Levesque's bright and engaging smiles of welcome.

'I shall be able to return later today, shan't I?' asked the dark woman with the Spanish look. She seemed anxious to make sure that her return was arranged. Lucille shook her head dubiously.

'I very much doubt it, Mrs Guay.'

The dark woman turned quickly to her husband, who was close behind her, and said in some alarm, 'In that case I shall have to cancel the trip, Joseph, if I can't get back.'

But this time Mr Guay was wearing a smile of his own. Both his words and manner were gently persuasive as Lucille Levesque heard him say to his wife, 'You must make the trip now it is booked and paid for, Rita. After all, if you can't get back, what does it matter? I can join you, and we can have a few days together. Don't you think that would be nice?'

The dark woman smiled in her turn and thought that would be very nice. Both husband and wife turned away from the ticket bureau as the call came for passengers to make their way to the waiting aircraft. Joseph kissed his wife and watched Rita walk to join the queue forming to go into the aircraft waiting on the tarmac. Soon the idling engines were revving up. The 'plane was a Dakota of Canadian Pacific Airlines, and the luggage had already been stowed and secured and the freight manifest cleared. The passengers were climbing into their seats. One group of men who kept together were American millionaires, all directors in a large US copper combine with considerable properties in Canada.

Joseph watched the blur of faces through the small windows as the doors were fastened. He waited for the 'plane to take-off, a curious feeling of mixed emotions possessing him. Occasionally he shifted his stance, but kept gazing at the aircraft as though willing it to become airborne. He stared at his watch.

Five minutes dragged by before the Dakota at last began to taxi down the runway. So it was five minutes late in getting away. Joseph Guay was perspiring as he turned his back on the September sunshine. He left the airport at a smart pace, the quizzical expression on his face rather anticipatory.

He was still on his way home when the Dakota blew up in midair. The wrecked aircraft nosed out of control, diving for the thick belt of forest land near Sault-au-Cochon, some forty miles beyond Quebec.

The first newsflash of the disaster reached the city an hour later. Joseph Guay, strangely, seemed rather like a man waiting impatiently for the terrible news. He hurried with his small daughter Lise, who was only five, to the airport. He was among the first of the group of anxious relatives bombarding the airline officials with questions.

He pushed his way forward to where a shocked Lucille Levesque had lost her customary smile, which was now replaced by a look of strain.

'Is the news true?' Joseph Guay inquired anxiously. 'Has there been a mistake—another 'plane—'

He broke off uncertainly.

'I'm sorry,' said Lucille in a dull voice. 'It's only too true.'

At that Joseph Guay appeared to break down. It was quite a histrionic performance. He clutched with groping hands at his small daughter, and surrendered himself to a grief that sounded and seemed inconsolable. He was so overcome that he had to be escorted to the Hôtel Château Frontenac, where he had a room booked for him. In his grief he seemed incapable of taking proper care of either himself or the little girl with him.

Perhaps that is why someone thoughtfully sent for a priest to render what solace and comfort he could to the husband and the wide-eyed child. Joseph was most assuredly not acting like a man who would benefit from the air disaster to the extent of ten thousand dollars.

Reports of the crashed aircraft claimed it had gone down in

one of the most inaccessible places in the province, and eventually it took a team of tough backwoodsmen working many hours to reach the wreck and bring out the twenty-three bodies. The tragic disaster was headline news throughout North America, and Canadian Pacific Airlines lost no time in getting experts onto the task of deciding the cause of the fatal accident. They were faced with claims amounting to millions of dollars.

The experts worked day and night without respite and in bad conditions. They started with the power units, for ground witnesses of the disaster claimed to have heard the engines running after the sound of the actual explosion in the sky. It seemed there was mystery to be explained. They found no sign of failure in the engines. Moreover, the state of the ground where the nose of the aircraft had ploughed into it suggested the airscrews were still turning at the moment of impact. In fact, the only sign of fire and scorched metal was in the freight compartment. Twisted pieces of metal from various parts of the freight compartment were cut out by oxy-acetylene, and some items of the baggage and freight were examined and chemically tested.

The chemists produced a shock for the airline company. They discovered minute traces of dynamite.

The accident, in short, had been no accident, but deliberate sabotage, which in turn meant multiple murder. But who could be capable of such a ghastly mass murder? It was a crime that had shocked the whole of Canada.

The mystery of what had happened to the Dakota, and why, was in due course handed over to the police. Detectives who had battled their way to the scene of the wreckage began their investigation by checking every consignment of freight against its listing on the company manifest. They also checked every passenger's background. They covered all freight except a single package consigned to New York and listed as a religious statuette. It had been boxed and wrapped in a brown paper parcel, and its weight was twenty-six pounds. An appeal to the woman who had delivered the package to the freight counter to come forward was broadcast. It was known she had been dressed in black.

Ten days after the disaster she had not been traced.

But on the tenth day Paul Pelletier came forward with a story about picking up a passenger for the airport. This passenger had been dressed in black. He gave the police the address of the house where he had collected her. It was found to be the home of Marie Petri, but when the Quebec detectives called it was to learn that Mrs Petri was in hospital. She was recovering from the effects of a large dose of sleeping pills she had taken, which could have been an attempt to commit suicide.

When she was able to talk to the officers at her bedside she looked scared and very subdued. When they asked questions she told them the story of being asked to take the religious figurine to the airport. The police probing continued until she told them about the promissory notes that were to be cancelled. The probing detectives learned that for a period of years Marie Petri had been the mistress of Joseph Albert Guay, a Quebec jeweller who was thirty-two years old. He had been latterly attracted to the charms of a younger and undeniably lovely girl named Marie-Ange Robitaille, who had a preference for turning her French christian names into their English equivalents of Mary Angel. To Joseph Guay she had been just Angel.

Yet such are the inexplicable relationships between lovers and ex-lovers, that even when Guay was enraptured with his new love, the plump Marie Petri remained on passing good terms with him, despite the hint of blackmail in the matter of the bank-held promissory notes.

Suddenly the plump woman who had dallied with suicide broke down. She was plainly on the edge of an emotional collapse, and the police were not willing to plunge her into its depths. They waited until she had calmed down, when she said miserably, 'I didn't know his wife would be on that 'plane.'

The Quebec detectives exchanged significant glances. They sensed they were close to something even more startling, so on the point of relaxing they kept up their stream of questions, and learned that a few weeks before Guay had rung up his one-time mistress with a strange request. He had wanted her to purchase for him ten pounds of dynamite, and offered a glib explanation. He wanted the dynamite sticks for a Mrs Cote who was anxious to have some rocks blown out of the ground of a property she had in the country. Marie Petri had accordingly ordered twenty half-pound sticks of dynamite. Mrs Parent, a friend of Marie Petri, had collected the dynamite for her, and Marie Petri had taken it to the restaurant where she worked. Guay had come in and taken it away.

Later the police decided they knew the source of the explosive that had wrecked the Dakota over Sault-au-Cochon, but they remained curious as to why the informant had taken that overdose of sleeping pills.

She remained silent after explaining that Guay had shown her a newspaper relating the search for the mysterious woman in black who had left an alleged statuette at the Ancienne Lorette Airport.

Then she said, 'He told me I wouldn't get away with any tale about a statuette,' and she went on to the listening detectives, 'He said I wouldn't be hanged after turning this trick—at least not by the neck. But by the feet—to make me suffer longer. He told me the best thing I could do for myself would be to swallow some sleeping pills and turn on the gas. He even told me I had better write a note saying I'd blown up the 'plane because I was jealous of him.'

The detectives stared at the woman.

'That is what you did, Mrs Petri?' inquired the detective asking the questions.

'Oh, yes,' she said in a husky whisper. 'I certainly tried—because—because . . .'

But when the tears came she couldn't continue.

When she finally left hospital the reporters and photographers were waiting in an eager group for her story. Cameras clicked as she looked strangely birdlike in her black coat and sleek black skull-cap. She was quickly dubbed 'Madame Le Corbeau' by the

French-language newspapers. The English-language journals followed suit, and in their columns she became known as 'Mrs Raven'. Once she realized how the publicity was treating her, she began demanding high prices for Press photographs. However, it was not long before the reporters and photographers were off on another scent for fresh copy.

The police had continued their inquiries and learned that Madame Le Corbeau had a crippled brother named Genereux Ruest, who was particularly adept at repairing fine mechanisms, such as clocks. This brother was paralysed from the waist down and had never walked. He propelled himself around in an invalid chair. Like his sister, he too had a story to tell. He told the police that Guay had come to see him about a week before the explosion aboard the Dakota. He had asked the cripple to make a time mechanism for him, rather like an alarm clock, that would detonate some dynamite.

According to the jeweller he wished to destroy some deep-rooted tree stumps. He had produced a clock face for the cripple to use as a time gauge. Ruest had fixed the mechanism as Guay had requested.

At this stage the police realized they had a case, for the mystery of what had happened to the destroyed 'plane could now be spelled out. Guay was arrested. The news was a sensation, and the cripple's contrivance supplied the Press with yet another label, for the mystery had now become 'The Love-Bomb Murder', and it was not to relinquish that title for many years.

Joseph Guay had sent more than twenty people to a terrible death just to be certain that he would be rid of the wife who stood between him and marriage to the woman who had inflamed his passion, the woman he called his Angel. When he appeared for the first time in a Quebec court, in October 1949, the public seats were packed, and crowds stood and waited in the streets outside.

Indeed, so great was the crush that it became an ordeal for the Provincial Police to bring the prisoner safely through the throngs to the court building. They looked like men expecting trouble, for one young man of eighteen, whose father had died in the disaster, had made headlines by publicly announcing that he was intending to take summary vengeance on the multiple murderer. He was arrested in order to prevent him attempting to carry out his threat.

The excited crowds thronging through the hilly town chanted their repeated hate against the prisoner.

'The dead must be avenged!' they cried in time to the chanting.

When Guay appeared there was a mass surge forward, but luckily the ranks of police held steady, or there could well have been a riot.

Guay had been charged with murder, and Marie Petri had been charged with attempted suicide, which was enough to hold her on while the full legal position was worked out by busy lawyers.

When the magistrates' hearing opened a new sensation was provided when an acquaintance of the prisoner came forward to tell the court of a curious conversation he had had, together with an offer of five hundred dollars. This witness's name was Lucien Carreau. Like most persons involved in this incredible case of mystery and violence he was a French-Canadian; indeed, the whole case had a strange and remote quality that stamped it as un-English. It was a typical *crime passionnel,* but with a difference. That difference was to make it unique.

In evidence Carreau told the court how one day Guay had come to him and explained how he was having a bad time with his wife. The two men were in Carreau's car at the time and he was driving through Lower Quebec. From a pocket Guay removed a bottle of cherry brandy and a small bag. He offered them to his friend, explaining that cherry brandy was Rita's favourite liqueur. In the bag was poison. He wanted his friend to put the poison in the cherry brandy, and later to offer Rita a couple of drinks from the bottle.

The crowd in the well of the court gasped. The story was

horribly consistent with others heard by the police and reported in the Press. It seemed that Joseph Guay was always on the look-out for a scapegoat to do his dirty work for him. In this case Carreau had turned to his companion and looked at him in amazement.

'Are you crazy?' he asked. 'I wouldn't get myself involved in such a racket.'

But Guay had persisted. He had offered a considerable bribe for his friend to join him in murder. However, Lucien Carreau had no outstanding promissory notes. His resistance to bribery could not be weakened. At the end of the car drive Guay still had his cherry brandy and his bag of poison.

There had been a minor sequel. When news of the Dakota crash had been broadcast, with pictures in the papers, Guay had again approached Carreau. This time the bribe was five times larger, as he wanted to buy his friend's silence. He was a man with a strange sense of relative values, probably because he placed an unreal one on his overwhelming passion for a younger woman with a face that drove him demented—he became obsessed with her. When he called on Carreau a second time with the increased bribe, his friend was becoming thoroughly scared by this business in which he had so nearly become involved through no wish of his own, and in which the other was still endeavouring to enmesh him.

'You can't buy me off, Joseph,' he had said bleakly.

Into court came another native of Quebec, Leopold Giroux, who had sold the sticks of dynamite to Mrs Petri. He was followed by Mrs Hector Parent, who had called for the parcel in order to oblige her friend Marie. The court of magistrates eventually decided that Guay had a case to answer, and he was formally committed for trial on the capital charge.

In the intervening months public interest in the case did not lag. 'The Love-Bomb Murder' continued to receive a wide coverage, as did any word about Mary Angel, who was portrayed as a veritable heart-throb and pictured as a *femme fatale*. She had not been called to give evidence in the magistrates' hearing, so she was seen as a mystery woman to most newspaper readers.

But Mary Angel was to provide her own measure of sensation when she gave evidence at Guay's trial, which opened in March 1950 before Judge Sévigny, with a snow blizzard sweeping Quebec. The day it opened the old Palace of Justice was crowded to the doors and the people turned away huddled together in the biting cold. But they would not leave.

The gum-chewing jeweller appeared and was escorted into the dock. He was now seen as a morose figure with an indrawn gaze and restless hands. His suit was creased and crumpled and his black bow-tie drooped like a broken wing. The crowds that had expected an early sensation were not disappointed, for the paralysed cripple, Genereux Ruest, had disappeared, and Judge Sévigny was asked by the prosecution to issue a court order for the witness to be found and held in custody. He was at last found forty miles away, and duly appeared and told his story of the request from Guay and of the mechanism he had contrived. The defence promptly asserted that it was impossible to make such a contrivance, but Noel Dorion, representing the Crown, called Professor Lucien Gravel of Laval University to explain that such a mechanism was quite possible.

Handed an alarm clock, he demonstrated how the mechanism could detonate a home-made bomb, as used in the Dakota disaster. It took him ten minutes to remove the minute hand of the alarm clock and connect a fuse and dry-cell battery. The hour hand was placed close to a screwed-down terminal. When they made contact the fuse was blown. Professor Gravel was asked how much dynamite, used in this way, would destroy a Dakota.

'Ten pounds of dynamite detonated by such a mechanism,' he replied, 'would be enough to wreck the interior of the 'plane and knock everyone aboard unconscious.'

Carreau then made a reappearance and related to the court how, after the disaster, the prisoner had described the death of his wife as a good riddance and had mentioned holding an insurance policy on his dead wife's life. By this time everyone was straining to get a glimpse of nineteen-year-old Mary Angel Robitaille, who was a cigarette-seller in the Monte Carlo Night Club, where she had met Guay. The most curious *ménage à trois* had evolved when the jeweller and the cigarette girl became lovers. Until then Marie Petri, who had worked in a restaurant, had satisfied the demands of Guay's extra-marital passion. But after meeting the girl in the night club the philanderer's standards had changed. He thought of himself as passionately in love. He was responsible for Marie Petri having the commodious apartment where she lived, and he told her bluntly he wanted to let another woman occupy a room. After an argument she had given way, and just occasionally he had returned to enjoy the charms of the older woman.

However, when Mary Angel appeared she was not quite the novelty that had been expected; in photographic parlance, she had been over-exposed to Press and public alike. Sixteen when she first met Guay, they had become lovers when he said his wife failed to understand him. She had accompanied him to a guest-house in Dorchester Street, Montreal, but Rita Guay had discovered the liaison and demanded that the girl's father do something about it. However, it wasn't the father who acted, but the daughter. Mary Angel moved into the room in Marie Petri's apartment, and changed her name to Nicole Cote. Marie Petri moved out, and the girl became a prisoner of her demanding lover.

She told the court, 'He wanted to get a separation from his wife, but said things were tough because he could find no grounds. He said he was going to have her watched to see if she was going around with anyone. At last common sense took the place of love, and I tried to get away from him.'

She borrowed twenty pounds, intending to reach Montreal, telephone her parents, and go back to them.

'I actually got on the train,' she explained, 'and a Negro attendant was making up my bed when Albert came running up.'

He took her luggage, dragged her from the train and shoved her into a parked car. He removed her footwear and they drove back to her prison room. After what she called a terrible scene she told him she still wanted to leave him. He flung her gloves into the stove. In the morning he tried to make amends with kisses. But his violence was savage, she recalled.

'He bit you?' asked Judge Sévigny.

'In a way,' she replied almost inaudibly. 'The marks remained for a week afterwards. He said it was so that I should not go out.'

Guay was now seen as a loathsome sadist.

After a see-saw existence they patched up their differences and Mary Angel got another night-club job, but again Guay stormed into her life, this time holding a gun.

'I was so scared,' she told the court, 'that I again went away with him to the Seven Isles. We went by 'plane.'

But his innate cruelty and sadism again manifested itself. They quarrelled and he struck her a heavy blow and left her out all night during a violent storm. By this time the court might well have asked if Guay was mad. The next piece of testimony makes one wonder, for after the girl had 'phoned her parents to ask them to send her money Guay had given her a letter. It was headed: 'To be thrown away after reading.' It was a wild protestation of his love in which he promised that he would soon be free of marriage.

It could be that the 'plane trip to the Seven Isles had sparked a fiendish plot in his mind, and he was certainly unbalanced. He told the girl that he wouldn't be able to see her until she was twenty-one, and asked her to wait for him, but by then he had something else to think about. Murder.

The defence put Mary Angel through a meat-grinder, and the grinding became very close-meshed when Mr Gerald Levesque asked her point-blank, 'Was that the first time you had relations with men—with Guay?'

'No,' whispered a very subdued witness.

But her morals, or lack of them, could not materially change the case as it affected the prisoner, and the jury seemed restless and ready to have the case concluded. They were absent only twenty minutes before returning with a verdict of guilty. The crowd seemed stunned, but Judge Sévigny told them, 'You have given a good verdict.' To the prisoner he said, 'For hatred of your wife, and as the result of your passion for your young mistress, you have perpetrated a diabolical, infamous crime.'

It was March 14th that Joseph Albert Guay, who preferred his mistress to call him by his second name, heard the sentence of death delivered, but he did not meet the hangman until January 10th, 1951.

He was only one of three who were executed for the wrecking of the Dakota. Marie Petri and her crippled brother had both been arrested and charged with complicity in the crime. By then the police had uncovered fresh evidence to satisfy a jury that they knew they were abetting a murderer. Ruest died on the scaffold where his sister's former lover had stood eighteen months before. A year later Madame Le Corbeau felt the hangman's noose tighten around her plump neck and suddenly realized that lust and love sometimes assume shapes of terror.

7

AUSTRALIA

The Clue in the Family Bible

Perhaps because it was a young country, brash, thrusting, and with a vigorous people, Australia around the time of the late eighteen-hundreds had a number of unusual and notable mysteries that came to baffle the police not only of its homeland, but also of the wider world in general.

One of these mysteries could be said to have its beginning in the year 1893, when New Year's Day was a sweltering time in the middle of summer in the suburb of Windsor, which was a part of the growing complex of Melbourne. It was shortly after Christmas that people in Andrew Street began complaining about the unsatisfactory state of the drains in the district.

'Where does that damned stink come from?' asked the station sergeant of several members of the police force.

'It's certainly spreading all over the neighbourhood,' one of his men told him. 'But I think, Sarge, it seems to be worst around the Drovens's house.' He added thoughtfully, 'By the way, you know they've moved out, don't you?'

The station sergeant looked at him and became interested. He made inquiries and learned that the Drovens were a couple not long out from England. The man had told neighbours that he was a toolmaker. The woman had said little enough. She was small and rather shy, with a quick and rather shuddering smile, as though she were afraid to allow anyone to see that she might wish to be pleased. A woman who had, so the gossips asserted, been afraid of her husband, a man with a sharp tongue and eyes that seemed never to change expression. Dead eyes with an intimidating stare. The menfolk in Andrew Street hadn't taken to him. As a familiar, or cobber, Droven was an unknown quantity, doing nothing to change his status, and on January 5th he handed over the keys of his house to the agent from whom he had procured them.

The sergeant became even more interested when he heard of the violent quarrel in the Drovens's house late on Christmas Eve. The windows had been shut, although it was a hot night, and the shouting and screaming disturbed people down the street. The sergeant found the notes made by a detective who had been to make inquiries about the commotion. A woman had told him that on the afternoon of Christmas Eve she had seen Mrs Droven for a short time in the garden.

'She looked terrible,' the detective had reported. 'She had a black eye and there were what looked like bruises on her face and neck. The woman I spoke to yelled across the fence to her. She ran indoors like a startled rabbit.'

The station sergeant decided to ask the house-agent to go and have a look at the Drovens's house. The man came away with a worried look.

'There's certainly a bad smell,' he agreed. 'I've been hoping it was drains and would just go.'

'You've been along to Andrew Street?' the sergeant asked.

'I went past, but didn't stop,' hedged the agent. 'The way things are arranged, when keys are handed over and a place becomes empty, I wait to hand the key to a likely tenant who wants a house in the district. But a couple who've been looking for a place says it doesn't suit them. Maybe it was the smell in this hot weather.'

In the event the police decided they had better investigate for themselves. They unlocked the front door and entered, but had no need to locate the stench. It met them in the small hall, a fetid odour emphasized by the close atmosphere of a house with all windows closed in hot weather. The smell seemed worse in the living-room, where one of the flagstones at the base of the hearth had at some time been removed and filled in with cement. The detective in charge of the station ordered the cement to be smashed. It was not thick. A few hammer blows cracked it, and the police cleared away the pieces to reveal the body of a young woman in a nightdress. She was young, and might have been pretty, but a blow from some heavy weapon had cracked her skull, and her throat had been cut.

The body was removed from the house and the air of Andrew Street became sweeter for the residents to breathe. Another detective squad arrived and searched the rooms and examined the furniture that had been left. They came upon a large family Bible. An inscription on the fly-leaf informed them that it had once been the property of Mrs Mather of Rainhill in Lancashire. It appeared to be the only clue to the identity or whereabouts of the absent Mr Droven. Inquiries were made throughout Melbourne, and a man answering to his description left a trail crossed by the dockside police. A man thought to be Droven had made inquiries about a passage to England. He had apparently gone to Sydney, and the manhunt switched to New South Wales. A man who might have been him had taken passage to England, using the name of Swanson.

However, there was no certainty at this time that he had actually sailed, and the police were in some doubt as to whether Droven had been laying a trail to mislead them. Inquiries for the arrest of a man answering to his description were sent to police throughout New South Wales and Victoria, while a cable was dispatched to England. It was thought that Mrs Mather of Rainhill should have some news.

In this way a world-wide hunt was begun in two places at the same time, twelve thousand miles apart, to discover anything about a man who had escaped from Australia in the name of Swanson or Droven, a man with staring eyes. Things happened in distant Lancashire with surprising swiftness. When the cable from Australia was received British detectives were soon calling on Mrs Mather, who still lived in Rainhill, and they mentioned a family Bible in which her name and address were inscribed. At mention of the Bible she pressed a hand quickly to her mouth and exclaimed in a choked voice, 'Oh, don't say something's happened to Emily!'

A hesitant story was unfolded. Emily was her daughter and the Bible was one Mrs Mather had given her before the young woman left for Australia with her husband. The pair had only recently been married. According to her mother Emily Mather had been starry-eyed and full of hope when she married Albert Williams on a fresh day in autumn. The date was the 22nd of September. Mrs Mather's eyes grew moist as she recalled the wedding and her own mixed emotions at the time.

'I couldn't help worrying a little,' she confessed. 'Emily seemed so fresh and untouched, if you know what I mean, and Albert, her husband, was a man of the world. I prayed that my girl would be happy, and that she had made the right choice for a husband.'

According to the story received by the Lancashire police after questioning Mrs Mather, Williams had been a comparative newcomer to Rainhill. He had descended on the locality some months before meeting Emily Mather. From reports he had seemed a rather flashy individual in the quiet Northern town, about four miles from St Helens which even today has only a few thousand inhabitants. He had rented a home in Lawton Road on a short-term lease, and made himself very approachable. At least, when he wanted to be.

He would lend an ear to anyone who would listen, and he seemed quite prepared to relate his adventures and the story of his travels in such distant parts of the world as the United States, Australia, and South Africa. He had been in the habit of dropping into one of the local hostelries and buying drinks in a somewhat patronizing way he had, which was felt by old-timers to be resented. At least, those of them who tried to dig beneath the surface of the man. He was, they saw, good-looking and over-ready to appear pleasant, with fair hair and complexion. Mrs

Mather put his age at around forty, which she had considered too old for a husband for her Emily, but seemingly the girl had been unable to resist the blandishments of the dashing figure cut by Albert Williams, with fashionable flowing whiskers and his London-tailored clothes.

'He was really too old for our Emily,' the mother insisted. Then she recalled that her visitors were detectives and became flustered. 'But what has happened? Why are you asking these questions?'

The Lancashire spokesman said, 'We've been asked to make inquiries, Mrs Mather. It's probably only a routine matter, but if there's any further news be sure we shall be calling on you again.'

When they left the modest house in Rainhill they knew that the woman who had given her family Bible to an emigrating daughter was filled with foreboding, but they left to make additional inquiries in the Lancashire town. What they were told seemingly justified the fresh anxiety felt by Mrs Mather for the girl in Australia. The detectives had a chat with a waitress in a local hotel. She told them that Bert Williams had spent a good deal of his time bragging in the bar and showing other customers some stones he claimed were uncut diamonds. She had once heard him talking about a fight he had with a pair of thugs who had set about him. If the story was to be credited, he had left the pair rolling on the ground and feeling grimly sorry for themselves.

The waitress's voice held a touch of scorn for a man with a big mouth and little to back it up.

'He talked big, and he acted big,' she declared about the absent man who had married a local girl, 'but I couldn't take to him. I didn't take to the way he looked women over, like they were cattle, nor the way he flashed his money. When he looked at me I felt I wanted to take a bath. But then it wouldn't do for us all to be alike, would it?'

She gathered up the glasses emptied by the detectives, and then leaned closer as she thought of an incident she suddenly recalled.

'I once asked him what his occupation was, for he seemed to

have a lot of time on his hands, and do you know what his reply was? "An inspector of regiments, my dear," he said without batting an eye. What the devil is an inspector of regiments? He had a twisted little smile when he spoke, I remember.'

Seemingly others in Rainhill had been given the same reply. It had not gone down too well. Possibly because his listeners had no idea what an inspector of regiments was any more than had the waitress. But on at least one occasion Williams had been constrained to let his viewers see for themselves what he meant, presumably believing in the old con man's axiom that seeing is believing.

So once he had appeared in the streets of Rainhill dressed in a garb none of the inhabitants had seen before. It looked like some kind of uniform and it was absurdly arresting by any yokel standards, for it was designed to be precisely that. It had been obtained from a London theatrical costumier, as was found out later when a whole jigsaw of puzzle pieces was put together by the police of two continents.

All in all, Albert Williams had gone to considerable trouble and not a little expense to dazzle the eyes of the Rainhill natives. He had descended on them like a being from another world.

To the suspicious detectives picking up the bits and scraps of news about him, that must have been his intention. He obviously believed in advertising himself. But to what purpose?

The mystery was not long in coming to a head.

He had already given out to those he considered his new-found cronies that he was in the Rainhill district on a house-hunting mission. His principal—whatever description that word was intended to imply—was a certain Colonel Brooks, who apparently wished to settle in the local area. The colonel had not visited Rainhill while Williams was there, and no one in the town had learned where the military gentleman resided or why he wished to come to that part of Lancashire, but it was in the name of this Colonel Brooks that Williams made arrangements to lease a comfortable residence in Lawton Road.

The colonel was most likely entirely fictitious, but the gossip about him and the free advertising he occasioned stood a plausible rogue in very good stead until his purpose was achieved.

Dinham Villa, in Lawton Road, was where Williams installed himself, while leaving the interested and very curious neighbours to suppose he was making final arrangements prior to the colonel's arrival. The whole conception was a charade. The villa had seven rooms and was a reasonably commodious Victorian dwelling-house, which Williams secured on a six-month lease at a rental of fifty pounds a year.

Knowing the value of inference, he announced that he was anxious to have in any signed agreements a clause that allowed the non-appearing colonel to renew his lease if he was satisfied with the villa as a home. The house-agent was very ready to promise that there would be no obstacle to an extension should it be desired.

Whoever Albert Williams was he was a glib-talking fake, and the police learned enough about him and his pretensions to recognize the manipulations of a con man. They went to visit Dinham Villa. The garden was overgrown and unkempt, with weeds invading the property, which was in a sad state and needed tidying up. The neighbours in Lawton Road and the tradespeople who had called at the villa while Williams was living there mentioned his married sister and her children. Seemingly she had arrived quite suddenly with her four offspring and stayed with her brother for a week.

The visit had caused much speculation around Rainhill, but at least it had allayed one rumour. Dubious believers in the mystery of Colonel Brooks's continued absence had been given something else to be intrigued about. They were wondering why Williams's sister and her children were never seen in the village. Albert Williams was quick to justify their non-appearance. He had explained his sister's not appearing in the small town by the fact that she was resting for some time while making arrangements for starting on a voyage to the United States. She was planning to go to Plymouth, from where the ship in which she had booked berths sailed. Her husband, he further explained, was in California, and the poor woman certainly had a considerable journey ahead of her which she was not looking forward to, especially as she was not a good traveller.

The sister was given quite a build up; and in the circumstances it seemed strange that she should elect to journey all the way up to Rainhill first, before going straight down to Plymouth. Moreover, her quartet of children remained absent with her, and as quiet as mice, which, when one came to ponder it, seemed both unnatural and extremely unlikely.

But like most of the facts pertaining to Albert Williams, the police found, they were inexplicably strange and bore no relation to the everyday. Indeed, the cautious inquiry he made of Dinham Villa's owner before he signed the six-month lease fell into the same category of strange, unusual, and very tall facts if one believed what one heard. Hearsay has a capacity to grow out of all proportion. That might have been something Albert Williams depended on.

He had insisted that the house-agent give him her address, and when he called on her, as the villa's owner, he was equally insistent that Colonel Brooks was a man seriously concerned about the level of the floors in any house he occupied. The poor woman was manifestly perplexed by his extravagant manner.

'The colonel, dear lady,' he had said, as though such a foible did not require an explanation, 'is unable to live in a house with uneven floors, and I'm afraid he would not approve of the floors in the kitchen and scullery at Dinham Villa, which is otherwise most suitable, I do assure you.'

The villa's owner might have been forgiven for wondering whether the absent colonel was really more concerned about stone-paved floors being cold and damp in winter and muggy weather. Anxious not to lose a tenant who might renew the lease for a considerable period if Williams was to be believed, she expressed herself as ready to have the kitchen and scullery of

Dinham Villa refloored with cement.

So Williams had signed the lease in the colonel's name, and the work was put in hand without delay. The fresh cement floor had been laid by Williams after he had taken over the occupancy of the villa.

But events were indeed about to overtake an unscrupulous and unconscionable blackguard who had contrived for far too long to have things his own way, and history was about to bring him his comeuppance in the present-day term. He had come a long way, but he was used to going to extreme lengths, and felt himself safe in simply running when the time was right, as he saw it.

In Dinham Villa a group of detectives met following Mrs Mather's news, and they stood in the stone-floored kitchen which had been cemented and walked around the floor, testing it for possible cracks or signs of weakness. The senior man stepped into the scullery, walked around again, and returned with a frown on his face.

'We'll have to have it up,' he decided, 'now we've come this far. It's never a pleasant job, and there's always the unexpected. So let's go to it, it won't be done by talking and staring at it.'

The men took off their jackets and began rolling up their sleeves with some mumbled muttering.

Following the example of the police in Melbourne, the Lancashire men attacked an area of cement flooring that was less well-laid than the remainder and less even. They made a great deal of noise and a considerable mess, and when the news of what was happening reached local inhabitants in Rainhill, a crowd gathered to watch the proceedings. Then reporters arrived on the scene. By this time the Rainhill crowd of sightseers and townsfolk had taken up positions around the villa, agog to witness the goings and comings of the police and the Press.

A notable absentee was Mrs Mather, who could not bring herself to join the crowd of expectant onlookers, and while she remained in her home she seemed very anxious to avoid any confrontation with the gentlemen of the Press.

As the hours passed there was a sudden stirring of excitement when a policeman wearing a shocked look left the villa with drying mud and cement on his boots and caking the bottoms of his dark blue trousers. He elbowed his way through the throng, and hurried to the nearest tobacconist's.

'I've been sent for some cigars,' he told the gaping shopkeeper. 'Better let me have the strongest you've got in stock.'

When he returned to the kitchen in Lawton Road his progress was followed by a straining sea of faces. The cigars were handed out to the shirt-sleeved constables resting on their picks and shovels. The window was open to clear a noisome stench. It came from a broken patch of cement rubble in the floor. The broken cement had been pushed back until the cigars arrived.

'We'll put this down to expenses,' said the senior officer, selecting and lighting one of the cigars being handed around.

Fortified with the cigars, the digging made fresh headway. The police stacked up the blocks of cement they had prised up and then they uncovered the first body. It was that of a baby that had been strangled. Their other discoveries were less pleasant. The woman's body was dressed in a nightgown. Her long dark hair draped her face like weeds. However, the features under it were sufficiently preserved to suggest that identification would be possible. Her bosom was dark with a scaly breastplate of dried blood. Her head had fallen back at an unnatural angle, for her throat had been cut. The three other children were like miniatures of their mother. Like her they were dressed in their nightclothes. They too had had their throats cut.

The crowd outside Dinham Villa remained long after the police diggers had gone and the bodies removed. When the police photos were circulated they brought a swift response from a couple of men; they called on the police and gave their name as Deeming. The man who had elected himself spokesman said, 'That woman found in the house at Rainhill, we think she's our brother Fred's wife. He married her twelve years ago, and we thought they were still living in Liverpool.'

The third brother had been known as Mad Fred by his family. His full name was Frederick Bailey Deeming. He had married a dark-complexioned girl who was Welsh. The wedding had been at Birkenhead in 1881. The two brothers spent a long while at the police station telling their listeners that the marriage of Mad Fred had been an unhappy one. The Welsh girl had done what she could for the sake of the children, but her husband had provided neither a decent home nor treated her with consideration as a wife.

'We talked to him,' the spokesman admitted, shaking his head, 'but it did no good. Besides, there were the kids to think of. Fred was just no good. That's the truth of it. No good and thoroughly selfish as well as work-shy. That summed up Fred.'

Before long cables were humming between England and Australia. The story that broke was a sensation, for Deeming alias Williams alias Droven had vanished under his latest name—Swanson. Before he was found and brought to trial a truly amazing career of fraud and violence was uncovered. It extended around the globe. He had first deserted the wife he murdered in Lancashire when he set sail for Australia in 1883. He was then about thirty, and had lived in Adelaide under the name of Ward before sailing in 1888 for St Helena and defrauding two brothers on the trip of sixty pounds. He arrived with his family in Cape Town, and, posing as manager of a diamond mine, began defrauding various jewellers not only in that city, but in Johannesburg and Durban. He was remembered in Klerksdorp for a gold mine swindle that netted him nearly three thousand pounds before he fled with his family to Aden en route to England, where he blazed a fresh trail of frauds from Hull to London and back to Stockton, then shipped out to Australia before doubling in his tracks again to North Africa and yet again returning to England.

The amazing saga of subterfuge and mystery continued in Yorkshire, where he had posed as a millionaire, and for a period in Belgium he became a nobleman named Dunn. He had been arrested in Montevideo, but later he arrived in Melbourne in the middle of December with Emily Mather and her family Bible in tow. He had put in a claim to the owners of the ship by which they had travelled from England for compensation for an alleged valuable necklace belonging to his wife which had been lost.

It could be seen perhaps as outraged justice that ordained a woman should provide the snare that tripped the agile feet that brought him retribution. Her name was Katie Rounsfell.

She made his murderous acquaintance on a ship sailing from Melbourne to Sydney. His inquiries into the sailing times for England had been a bluff, as had a visit to a Melbourne matrimonial agency; when later in Sydney she inquired where they were headed, and he told her they were off to the goldfields, her eyes widened, for when he had first met Katie he told her he had secured a post with Fraser's mine, the fabulous Southern Cross. He said he was starting out again and she should come out and join him. To the Australian girl it sounded like an invitation, but while she hesitated in Sydney the news of Emily Mather's body being found in Melbourne sent a shocked young woman hurrying to the police.

Her story was handed to Sergeant Considine, in charge of the Melbourne end of the intercontinental investigation. Considine produced a thick dossier on Frederick Bailey Deeming, which eventually included reports of the bodies of several women being found in houses he had rented in Johannesburg. To date Deeming had been responsible for the known deaths of six persons, two women and four children, and possibly for three or four more women. The mystery of their deaths remained, but a very sober Katie Rounsfell felt she had had a narrow escape.

Considine wired the police in Bathurst, and one day at Fraser's mine, when he least expected it, a hand fell on the wanted man's shoulder.

'I'm arresting you for the murder of Emily Mather at Windsor,' said a detective.

Swanson, as he called himself, tried to bluff it out, but it didn't work for him this time. He was transferred to Perth on the way back, where he admitted he was Williams, but swore that he hadn't killed Emily. He had been wearing a full moustache when he arrived in Perth. One morning it was missing, and he had not been allowed a razor. It is believed he had scraped the whiskers from his upper lip with a piece of broken glass to make recognition in Melbourne less certain. Considine had sent a detective named Cawsey to collect his prisoner in Melbourne, and Cawsey was accompanied by a man named Hirschfeldt, who had been a passenger on the ship taking Emily Mather to a new life, as she had supposed.

As soon as Cawsey's companion saw the prisoner he recognized the man with staring eyes.

'That's Bert Williams, as his wife called him,' he nodded. 'They were down on the passenger list as Mr and Mrs O. A. Williams.'

The arrest was cabled to England. A Scotland Yard senior detective took passage to Australia, where after several weeks following his arrival a conference was held. It was decided that in the unlikely event of Swanson or Bert Williams or Droven cheating justice by being found not guilty in Melbourne, then he would be extradited to Britain and charged with the murder of the dark-complexioned Welsh girl he had hauled around the world with their growing brood before he induced her to pose as his sister prior to cutting her throat and the throats of his older children and strangling the baby.

There was going to be no way out for the killer to cheat justice this time. Indeed the mills of the gods were beginning to grind exceeding small for Frederick Bailey Deeming, as his brothers knew him.

The State of Victoria, however, was jealous of its reputation. Deeming would have to provide unquestionable proof of his innocence if he was to keep his neck out of a noose made from Australian hemp. The man kept locked in a cell thought he had one chance of winning sympathy in Australia. That was by keeping Katie on his side, but even then he couldn't resist referring to money. He wrote her a badly mis-spelled letter, for he was practically illiterate despite so many pretensions to wealth and quality. In this he stressed his innocence and told her that his feelings for her were unchanged and daily brought him comfort. He appended his little piece, first trotted out at Fraser's mine, about many an innocent man being hanged these days, and told her that if she would not marry him life would not be worth the living. At the very end of this indifferent missive he scrawled his signature, and then requested that she send him money to help with the cost of his defence. If she hadn't any she might sell some rings he knew she had and send on the cash from their sale.

The colossal humbug had a skin like a pachyderm.

If he had been visiting royalty the crowds that gathered to meet his ship and train on the journey to Melbourne could not have been greater. But the shouting held the wrong kind of enthusiasm. Some of them tried to lynch him. At Adelaide an elderly woman was so fascinated by her proximity to a man she was sure was a multiple killer that she came back several times to stare at him as he sat at a train window. This enraged him and he threw whisky in her face. In Melbourne fifty witnesses identified him, not always correctly, for it was established that he had used fifteen aliases.

When he realized he had no chance of being acquitted he feigned insanity, and during the trial assured the jury that both his parents had been in an asylum, which was why he had been nicknamed Mad Fred. But in this connection one of the doctors who attended him in prison had something else to tell the jury.

'Deeming,' he said, 'frequently spoke of his mother, declaring she appeared before him every morning, and during one of her appearances in Sydney she told him to kill every lady friend he had.'

Before the jury retired he made an abusive speech.

'I haven't had a fair trial,' he shouted. 'It's not the law that's trying me, but the Press. The case was prejudiced even before my arrival by the exhibition of photos in shop windows, and it was by means of these that I was identified. I leave it to the jury to say that it is not the case that there are hundreds of people in

Melbourne who would execute me without trial. If I could believe that I had committed murder I would plead guilty rather than submit to the gaze of the people in this court—the ugliest race of people I have ever seen.'

Australians never forgave him those last words.

The jury found him guilty and added a rider that they did not find him insane. It was their way of making finally sure of the outcome.

He was sentenced to death, and the Privy Council in London refused a stay of execution, and he was accordingly hanged on the 23rd of May, 1893, in Melbourne.

8

AMERICA

Was Starr Faithfull Murdered?

One of the enduring mysteries of New York occurred nearly fifty years ago and despite several attempts to graft a solution on to the mystery it remains unsolved, and the likelihood is that it will remain so, just as there is no answer to the riddle of what happened to Muriel McKay at Rook Farm—unless eventually someone talks out of turn. In the case of Starr Faithfull and the half-century that has elapsed that is now only a remote possibility which has admittedly become merely academic. However, the essential mystery continues to puzzle all who are attracted to an unsolved enigma surrounding possible murder.

Starr was a playgirl almost as soon as the word was coined in that decade following the First World War. In London, which she visited, she might have been termed a Bright Young Thing, and with reason. She glowed like a meteor intent on burning up space.

However, her mother had given her a head start when Starr was christened, for she was given a name that sounded like a concocted Hollywood creation. Actually it was her own, but the mystery of what happened to her has helped to commemorate it, for it is one of those names that, once heard, is not readily forgotten. Her mother had married a retired chemical manufacturer, Stanley E. Faithfull, after her divorce from Starr's natural father, Frank Wyman. On her mother's second marriage the girl adopted her stepfather's name, and by the time she was twenty-five she had blossomed and matured into a young woman of good looks and some claim to beauty.

The family home was by this time in St Luke's Place, Greenwich Village, where in later years the latter-day Bohemians forgathered to exchange beads and amulets and even wives and husbands. Some sold 'grass' among the Flower People, for the world was not only changing, but growing used to the changes. Starr herself was a complex character, with a peculiar mixture of thrills and dreams in her life, as well as intense likes and strange dislikes. In fact, she seldom knew what her preferences were for long, either in emotions or in men. She was at times hilariously happy, at others plunged into the depths of dejection. She was, not surprisingly, hard to live with, and her parents came to think of her as someone who could be unpredictable and at times difficult.

Perhaps this is why, on a June Saturday in 1931, Stanley Faithfull had gone to the police to report that his stepdaughter was missing from home. She had left St Luke's Place at nine-thirty the previous day in the morning, June 5th. She had gone out, as her parents believed, to do some neighbourhood shopping, but had failed to return.

'Has she made a habit of such disappearances?' asked a station sergeant who was taking notes.

'No. This is the first time,' said Stanley Faithfull, looking worried. 'Her mother is anxious, as you can well understand.'

The sergeant, who had heard many stories about missing persons, nodded sympathetically.

'All right,' he said, 'we'll make inquiries for her, Mr Faithfull. Chances are she will soon be back with you. Most of them find their own homes are best, but they have to find it out for themselves.'

However, when the first inquiries produced no result the police agreed to have Starr Faithfull's full description broadcast, with details of what she was wearing at the time she had left home. She had not been wearing any pieces of jewellery and had only three dollars in her handbag. The detailed description of the wanted girl was duly broadcast, but only a short while afterwards a girl's body was found on the sands of Long Beach, Long Island. It had been rolled over in the tide and held some disfiguring bruises which made the police officer who discovered her narrow his eyes.

There was no ready means of identification until the arrival of Stanley Faithfull. He gulped as he removed the sheet covering her marked face, and took a long breath which was like an indrawn sigh.

'Yes, that's my stepdaughter,' he choked, and a glaze like a cataract descended over his sight.

He turned, and the police led him away. The body was taken to the Nassau County mortuary, where a doctor named Otto Schultz examined the remains and later performed a post-mortem. He reported that she had met her death by drowning, but he had found that she had been criminally assaulted. Her limbs and trunk bore witness to substantial bruising, and there were visible marks which had been made before death. On the other hand, some of the bruising had occurred after death. The doctor was in a quandary about some of the marks found on the body. He felt that although she might have been physically assaulted, some of the bruises could well have been caused by contact or collision with a heavy object during the time the body was in the water.

The official verdict on Starr's death was described accordingly as submersion or drowning. But the mystery of how that came to be was enhanced when it was discovered that sand was present in her throat and lungs. This indicated that she had died in shallow water, which provided a fresh puzzle, for Starr Faithfull had been a strong swimmer and had not been subject to cramp when swimming.

Consequently the medical examiner was in two minds about the death. He, too, consulted the police. They were divided in their opinions as to the cause of the girl's death. One group believed she had been murdered. The other felt that she had committed suicide. Either opinion contained the ingredients of mystery at a time when the bereaved parents decided to have Starr's body cremated. They were actually kneeling down during the service in the chapel when the proceedings were stopped by a court order. The cremation ceremony was abruptly halted.

The reason given for the interrupted ceremony was ostensibly to give independent witnesses an opportunity for identifying the remains. They were suspected of being those of a woman who had been seen in what were termed suspicious circumstances. The police also wanted to know if she had been a passenger who engaged certain taxis. The interrupted ceremony of course resulted in a great deal of publicity, which did not evaporate when the cremation was held twenty-four hours later and the suspicions of the police were seen to be unfolded, but at least so far as Starr was concerned not unproven, for now a large query had been attached to her name, which would continue to grow.

The Press publicity resulted in three men being singled out to discover how Starr Faithfull had died and possibly why. This trio of investigators included two police chiefs, Chief Abram Skidmore and Chief of Detectives Harold King. They worked with the county prosecutor, Elvin Edwards. For his part, King had acquired a considerable reputation. He was claimed to be one of the best crime solvers in the United States. The three investigators soon concentrated on the murder aspect; suicide was thought to be too easy a conclusion. So they began delving into Starr Faithfull's past.

They learned that in the spring the young woman had been attacked and beaten up in New York by a man registered in a hotel. She had been rushed to hospital, where she was found to be suffering from alcoholism in an acute state. A day later she had been released in the custody of her parents, while her attacker had been released for an unknown reason, although Starr had sustained contusions of the jaw and face.

She made a formal statement about the incident.

'I had been drinking gin,' she said, 'as far as I know. This is the first time I had drunk anything for six months. I don't know how many I had. I suppose somebody knocked me about a bit.'

Gradually the outer wrapping was taken off a cover-up story and the popular Press worked it into large headlines. Now, like the trio of detectives, they were really digging, and felt they had something to dig for. The Starr Faithfull story continued to grow in interest and coverage. It was learned that in 1925, six years before, she had been a patient in the Channing Sanatorium at Wellesley, where she had been admitted under the hybrid name of Starr Wyman. She was discharged nine days later under the brief word 'Improved'.

However, with the mystery of her death continuing to grow and broaden, Skidmore and King learned that she had sailed for London in the autumn of 1930, with enough money in her handbag this time to pay for new clothing and trips into London's West End, where she visited a number of night-clubs. On one occasion she is reported as having danced naked in a pub in the Fulham Road, while the man who was her escort at the time was so angry with her that he drew a gun and fired into the ceiling. A couple of women rushed her into the women's room, quietened her down and then dressed her. She returned to the bar as though nothing had happened.

This made compulsive reading in the New York papers, particularly when they learned that a couple of years earlier, in 1928, Starr had attempted to destroy herself because one of her love affairs had gone wrong. She was prevented from going through with the act by a chambermaid. But now the picture of the woman from Greenwich Village was being radically changed in the Press accounts of her life and death. It was made into a piquant serial story.

Because of the growing lapse of time the original theory that Starr had been murdered gradually lost impact; the general feeling of New Yorkers was that she had been a wild one and probably got what she asked for. But the trio of investigators were not satisfied with any halfway measures. They had had teams out looking over miles of Long Island beaches for the girl's missing clothing, while her family had gone through letters and diaries that might provide a clue. The investigation even took into account titles of crime books found in her home. They were all mystery novels and detective stories, with the single exception of a lone volume of Tennyson. It was this last that provided a real surprise.

Hidden behind that volume of Tennyson's collected works was a slim book bound in silk. When the detectives opened it they realized they had found the woman's diary.

It was in longhand, with characters not open and widely-spaced, but rather cramped and narrow, and the contents held personal vignettes of people and places as well as the writer's impressions upon events and happenings. The diary with dates covered a period of about four years. One of the first things Elvin Edwards did was to have an acknowledged handwriting expert compare the writing in the diary with known samples of Starr Faithfull's hand.

The writing was pronounced to be identical.

But one authority who studied the contents of the diary felt that if anything it tended to strengthen the suicide theory. He based his new assumption on the general tone of the written words. They seemed to indicate that the writer was a person who had endured despair without finding a satisfactory outlet for her secretly recorded emotions. Certain words and phrases recurred repeatedly, such as the 'futility of life' and even 'suicide'.

But after the diary had been perused and studied there emerged clear indications that there might be a sequel or second volume. The hunt for such a follow-up volume of the diary eventually extended across the Atlantic, from New York to London, where Starr had upon occasion kicked over the traces in expressing herself as a liberated young woman. The man who came upon the second book of Starr Faithfull's diary was a London hotel manager. He explained to the patient New York detective making inquiries how he had come to find the diary.

'She came to my hotel,' he said, 'with two Innovation trunks packed with expensive clothing. Two days later she disappeared without paying her bill, but leaving her luggage behind. I searched it to try to trace her, and found the diary.'

The two volumes of the diary recorded a day-to-day account of Starr's affairs and love adventures from the day she had left school. She had made no secret of her intention to tell the truth about herself in her writing.

As the London hotel manager explained somewhat ruefully, 'Some of the entries were so frankly intimate that I locked the diary in my private safe to prevent it from being seen by our staff. Subsequently a banker's draft came from America, clearing up her bills, and I released her luggage, placing the love diary back in it.'

However, the mere mention of something that had been described as a love diary was enough to send the New York journalists and reporters on a new hunt for background information and fresh stories. Certainly the finding of the second volume had provided the mystery with additional material, for this was the volume that provided the juiciest extracts from an intemperate love journal.

The pressure on Starr's parents became too much for the couple, and they made a fresh statement to the Nassau County authorities about their dead daughter. This was to bare other skeletons in the family's closed closet. Elvin Edwards was now told that when she was a young girl of eleven the daughter had been seduced by a man old enough to be her father, and this experience had produced a marked effect on her in her later formative years.

'Starr was a different person after that,' said her mother.

She had decided that following the experience Starr should be put in a sanatorium, but this had only worked in the short term, for some days after she had been released she was rationalizing what had happened as due to a romantic interlude with a boy in her own age group. But seemingly the damage had been done, and Starr remained an unsettled person during most of her teens.

Her father had decided that a Mediterranean cruise might do her good, and certainly when she returned to the United States as a young woman of nineteen she seemed to be improved in spirits and outlook. It was in the mood of baring the truth and clearing away the deadwood of the past that she confided to her mother the deeper relations she had had with the man who had seduced her. He had induced her to read for him passages from the pages of a well-known writer of sexy books, and she had been excited by the vicarious descriptions of the love acts. In this way she had been introduced to the acts themselves.

This confession had appalled her parents, who had in consequence consulted a lawyer, and as a result Starr was given both medical and psychiatric treatment. Because of the expense entailed the Faithfulls felt that the man himself should contribute to their daughter's rehabilitation. Legal negotiations were begun which dragged on until the man finally settled any remaining claim upon Starr and her parents for twenty-five thousand dollars. He was released from any further obligation.

However, this particular passage through Starr's formative years was a bumpy one.

There was the occasion when Starr returned home from a meeting with a man who was a ship's doctor. They had quarrelled and the doctor became so angry that he declared that he never wished to see her again.

Starr had told her mother acrimoniously, 'Well, he never will again, I can assure you.'

Up to the death of the girl in the waters of Long Island Sound nothing had been published about the settlement of the twenty-five thousand dollars paid by the man who had seduced her as a child. But shortly after discovery of Starr's body someone had got in touch with the attorney of the man who had so drastically influenced a child's life. So now that Starr Faithfull was dead there was an attempt to secure more money, but just how this endeavour collapsed, or why, was not made very clear.

But Starr had a unique way of leeching on to persons to whom she mattered, as the closing episode of the ship's doctor demonstrates. On June 23rd some related testimony was produced. This consisted of some love letters written to him by the dead girl between May 30th and June 4th, 1931. In a couple of them Starr had definitely affirmed her intention to commit suicide, and as the police proved, there was no doubt that these letters were in Starr's own handwriting, although her family was by this time contending that they were nothing more than forgeries.

In one—her last to the doctor—she had penned:

'It is all up with me now. This is something I am going to put through. The only thing that bothers me about it, the only thing I dread, is being outwitted and prevented from doing this—which is the only possible thing for me to do.'

Then she said a strange thing as she went on:

'When one wants to get away with murder one has to keep one's wits. It is the same way with suicide. If I don't watch out I will wake up in a psychopathic ward, but I intend to watch out and accomplish my end this time. I want oblivion. I am going to drink slowly, keeping aware of every second. Also I am going to enjoy my last cigarette. It is a great life when one has twenty-four hours to live.'

But what did she mean, and what were her intentions? That mystery has never been solved.

For although the medical authorities had stated her death had been due to drowning, just how she drowned or why has never been clearly understood. For instance, why had none of her clothes been found? If there had been an accident, why had she not struck out, like the strong swimmer she was known to be, and saved herself?

There remains a residue of curious facts. For instance, on June 5th, the day that Starr disappeared in St Luke's Place, the vessel on which the ship's doctor was cruising sailed for the Bahamas. A cab driver claimed that late in the afternoon of the same day he drove Starr and a man from the docks. The woman was the worse for imbibing. He had added that she had returned alone to the dock. They then set off again, but drove only a short distance.

'I've only got ten cents,' she said, and climbed back out of the cab.

But the significance of this story could not be assessed, for upon occasion she had made a habit of visiting transatlantic vessels while they were docked in port and called to see officer friends. It has even been theorized that she might have been in a disturbed state of mind and when an ocean-going vessel passed through the Narrows she had jumped overboard in the darkness, though on a June night there would have been plenty of light. In that case, what became of the girl's clothes, including undergarments and shoes?

And what of motive?

The crime, if there was one committed, would appear to be motiveless with the exception of the unknown or his associates who were attempting to raise money by possible extortion. This theory has been called far-fetched.

Perhaps any theory that has been considered in the past fifty years must be labelled in the same way—far-fetched. But the fact remains that Starr Faithfull died, yet she was not known to be a drug addict, though at times she certainly indulged in excessive drinking, even for a young woman, but there was nothing in her two volumes of diaries to suggest her alcoholism was any more than the result of mood and depression.

On the other hand, because a perpetual query must remain against what happened to her one has to consider at least the possibility of some unknown factor, what might be called the X factor so loved of detective-story writers demanding a neat conclusion. But there was no neat conclusion for Starr. It was open-ended and untidy.

Certainly the Press made the most of the mystery girl who shocked both London and New York in her day, but although reporters started numerous hunts of their own the various leads all came to nothing.

Yet the mystery of how Starr came to be without her top clothes, undergarments, and shoes is something that challenges all conception of what is known about her and came to be revealed in her extraordinarily frank diary. It is true that she could have drowned, but then what of the bruising to her body?

In the months following the excitement occasioned by the revelation of her diary the tabloids went to town to try to outvie the police in coming up with an extravagant solution to what looked like being one of New York's unsolved mysteries. Indeed several books were later written about the mystery, but on each occasion the writer was forced to concede that the full truth had not been revealed and that the mystery remained tantalizingly out of reach of a final answer.

But even in the realm of speculation the excavators digging for pay dirt, as they considered, were not rewarded by so much as a gleam of the hidden truth. A number believed that on that last day in her life Starr may have boarded a ship about to depart from New York, and the story of the cab driver was given great prominence over large-sized headlines. A number of bright suggestions were given flower, but they were doomed to wither as blooms when the story was examined and re-examined. But it is true that someone whose identity Starr had not revealed for her own reasons might have secretly joined her in an illicit relationship of which he had tired.

It is possible as speculation that the man had grown annoyed by Starr's hounding him, and finally he had come to the point of solving the problem she had created. He might have made sure that Starr was unobserved when she joined him on a ship about to sail. To ensure that she did not wander about the decks he could have encouraged her to have disrobed. She could have been part-way drunk, and as darkness fell it would not have been difficult for him to have carried an unclothed and unprotesting female who was intoxicated to the rail of the ship unobserved and dropped her over the side.

Some such exit must have been made by Gay Gibson, the English girl who vanished on board the *Durban Castle*, homeward bound from Cape Town to Southampton, sixteen years later, in

1947. But in her case the man responsible for dropping her overboard was known. If this was Starr Faithfull's fate on a June night after darkness had fallen the man who dropped her body overboard remained unknown.

Had she brought her diary up to date there might have been a grimmer story to tell of intrigue and pervading motive.

It was theory at best, and even somewhat wild, although no wilder than some of Starr's own erotic episodes in the past decade of her strange and wayward life. But there are some apparent weaknesses in the theory. Any murderer contemplating Starr's removal from the ship would have been running some incredible risks so shortly after sailing time. He would have insisted on concealment, helped by Starr's disrobing, but one thing was sure, in that case. It was not a casual pick-up on the part of either of them. They had come to know each other and there had been other times when they had enjoyed what the tabloids of the early 'thirties termed illicit sex, with all its permutations.

Other factors had to be considered for any man contemplating the disposal of a woman at sea, even if she had been too drunk to swim, and a dousing of cold water might have well revived her, though that could have been allowed for. The activity and bustling hurry of both stewards and passengers settling down for a voyage would have meant running a very great risk, with personnel checking cabins and passenger lists, all part of the regular procedure for making sure that there were no stowaways on board.

But a determined man might well have been prepared to run this desperate kind of risk. Certainly the condition of Starr's body when found on the Long Island sand with marked bruising and battering suggested that it had been tossed about in a heavy swell or by waves. It could even have been in collision with some weighty object such as a heavy bulk of timber or other flotsam.

However, the record of the post-mortem stands, from which it is not likely that Starr was beaten insensible by a murderer or that she was carried much of a distance by a man bent on disposing of her body. There was of course no evidence that she had been drugged, though this cannot be completely ruled out. Once entering this particular field of speculation the scope is considerably widened, for she could have been drugged and taken out in a power-boat for disposal. But then comes an edgy return to motive.

Starr Faithfull had never been one to cover her tracks smoothly or easily. She had been too intent on her short-term objectives. There also remains the possibility that her murder, had it occurred, had been accidental. In that case the killer must have been confounded by the prospect of what to do with her body, for he would not want to leave any clues that might lead to himself or what he had done.

But who can say how a murderer by accident will react?

He may not be a calculating or cohesively thinking person and perhaps he would have tossed the body into the sea as the one way of being rid of it—until it returned naked to the stretch of sandy coast, where searching police found it.

So the riddle of her death remains and continues to intrigue generations of readers to whom she was a stranger whose story for a time made large headlines and bedevilled men who tried to find a solution to the mystery without being successful when they called a halt to their investigations.

In the same way the riddle of what happened when Julia Wallace was beaten to death in Liverpool remains an unsolved mystery of the same period. Indeed, of the same year. For the English wife was murdered on the 19th of January, 1931, while Starr Faithfull's body was found on Long Beach nearly six months later in the same year.

But in other respects their stories are very divergent and dissimilar. Indeed one cannot be sure in the case of the American woman that crime was indeed committed. But there has never been any doubt about how the English middle-aged matron met her death. She was bludgeoned to death on her own hearth.

'Perhaps the most remarkable thing about the murder of Julia

Wallace,' commented the late Dorothy L. Sayers, with whom I once discussed the case, 'is that from the beginning to end there was no important conflict of evidence.'

Nor was there in the case of Starr Faithfull.

But both cases left plenty of scope for conjecture.

9

ENGLAND

The Address that Never Was

William Herbert Wallace was a married man of fifty-two who lived a quiet life with no ostentation or show. He was an agent of the Prudential Insurance Company with savings of just over a hundred and fifty pounds and his income amounted to two hundred and fifty pounds per annum. From this it may be deduced that he and his wife Julia lived very modestly in their terrace house in a suburb of Liverpool. They had no children. At the back of the house there was a paved yard, and in the front a metre or so of turned-over earth that was usually referred to as the garden. It was a sanctuary where cats scratched and lurked on the lookout for mice.

It was the home of a drab couple with no pretension to personality or ambition. They were content to arrive in this working-class backwater and shelve any ambitions they might have had and let the world pass them by so long as it made no demands on them. Their friends and acquaintances were few and they had few social inclinations and in the main kept themselves very much to themselves. The husband was considered to be what was called a quiet little man, but his wife had at one time bloomed in their younger years to become a passable pianist and to paint in water-colours. She had once learned French. Wallace himself was of a more 'modern' bent. He had lectured upon occasion in chemistry at the Liverpool Technical College. He also played chess, though he was no grand master, and he kept a diary. He was even learning to play the violin, and he hoped in time to play duets with Julia.

All things considered, it was a very circumscribed and normal existence before the days of television, when individuals had to make their own entertainment or else let time hang heavily on their idle hands. Their life had assumed a pattern with neither valleys nor slopes, and it progressed from day to day at a placid tempo, and, to be quite honest, that was how they wished it to be.

That is not to say that neither had secret longings for change, but so far as is known they remained unexpressed and secret.

'We lived in perfect harmony,' said the husband, 'for sixteen years. Our days and months and years were filled with complete enjoyment, placid perhaps, but with all the happiness of quietude.'

Herbert Wallace was given to creating the odd fine phrase for effect. But on a January day in 1931 he found himself speechless. His liking for any phrases, ugly or fine, evaporated like steam. He had gone out to find a non-existent address and returned home to find that his front door would not open, because the bolt had been shot, presumably by his wife, as he had warned her to bolt the front door when alone in the house after dark. He walked to the back door, and found that also would not open. He then banged on the door, using his fist, but got no ready answer, which surprised him, for he did not think Julia would have slipped out to go to the post. But of course she might have become drowsy and fallen asleep by the fire. He was about to make sure that the back door had not simply become stuck, as it sometimes did in cold weather when the wood swelled, when he heard his next-door neighbours coming out of their back door.

They were a Mr and Mrs Johnston. The woman recognized him in the poor light, and said pleasantly, 'Good evening, Mr Wallace.'

He acknowledged the greeting and then said on the spur of the moment, 'You haven't heard anything unusual tonight?' with a query in his voice.

The woman turned and said with some surprise, 'No. Why? Has anything happened?'

He said he couldn't get into the house.

'Try again,' said Johnston, and reminded Wallace that the doors all had the same key. 'I'll fetch mine if you like.'

Within a couple of minutes he had brought his own back door key. It turned easily and Wallace went in, calling, 'Julia? You there?'

But his wife did not reply, which seemed strange, so he hurried upstairs in the dark, still calling to her, wondering if she had gone to lie down while he was out. The bed was still unmade, which was unusual; he hurried downstairs in the dark, and struck a match to light the gas. There was a slight plop as the mantle flared and an incandescent glow spread over the room.

He stared in horror. For some moments the only sound in the room was the soft hiss of the gas.

When his gaze cleared he stared at the pool of blood and saw the wound in his wife's head. He knelt by the hearth and tried to feel her pulse. His fumbling fingers felt no throb. A blind instinct made him stagger to his feet and totter away. He reached the back door he had so recently shut, and flung it open. The Johnstons heard him and looked up.

He called to them, 'Come and see! She's been killed!'

He had prided himself on being a man who kept his cool, as the modern phrase has it, but when he stared at the Johnstons he heard his voice crack as his neighbours led him into the kitchen. There was brief talk about the possibility of a burglar having broken into the house, and Wallace began looking about him to see if anything was disturbed or missing. But he felt drawn to the place where his wife lay, and he bent over her. Then he saw the mackintosh on which his wife was lying. He recognized it. By this time Mrs Johnston was becoming agitated due to the shock of the discovery.

'The fire's out,' she said. 'Perhaps we should light it.'

The next minutes passed in slow progression until Wallace said he must call the police. Soon a knock came at the front door, and Wallace opened it to an overcoated officer. 'Something terrible has happened,' he said. Together they entered the room where his wife lay and saw the blood and Julia's battered head. 'How did this happen?' asked the officer, looking at Wallace, who said with a shiver, 'I don't know.'

The policeman took out his notebook and asked for details about where he had been and what he had done since he left home, and Wallace began a curious story. He had caught a tram, but had been uncertain about his destination, and he had asked the conductor if this tram took him to Menlove Gardens East. The conductor shook his head.

'No,' he said. 'You should change to another car further on.'

Wallace duly changed cars, reminding the conductor as he punched the ticket, 'You won't forget I want to go to Menlove Gardens East, will you?'

When the tram dragged to a halt Wallace alighted.

'Here you are,' said the conductor. He watched the passenger reach the kerb, then rang the bell. The tram moved sluggishly on, and Wallace began looking for the address he had been given. It was 25 Menlove Gardens East.

But he couldn't find it. He walked to Menlove Gardens West and found himself in a foreign neighbourhood. Seeing No. 24 Menlove Gardens West, he knocked on the door and inquired if a Mr Qualtrough lived there. A stranger looked at him and shook his head.

'I've never heard of Menlove Gardens East,' he told the inquiring agent of the Prudential, and Wallace suddenly realized he was adrift in the city of Liverpool.

The mystery began when he entered the City Café, where the Liverpool Chess Club held regular meetings. The club's captain, Samuel Beattie, approached Wallace soon after he had begun a new game and said he had a 'phone message. Wallace looked up inquiringly. 'It's from a man named Qualtrough,' Beattie explained. But Wallace shook his head. He said, 'I've never heard of him. Who is this Qualtrough?'

'He wants to meet you tomorrow evening at seven-thirty, at 25 Menlove Gardens East. Something to do with your business. I suggested he ring later,' said Beattie, 'then he could speak to you himself. But he said he couldn't manage it. Something about his daughter's twenty-first birthday party.'

The two men stared at each other.

'Menlove Gardens East,' repeated Wallace. 'It must be somewhere near Menlove Avenue.'

He returned to his chess game, which he won about two hours later, then he went home, where he told Julia about this new inquiry. The next day he was caught up in insurance business and did not think of Menlove Gardens East until later in the evening. Being a man who preferred to deal with events as they arrived he decided to venture out that evening to call on this Mr Qualtrough whoever he was.

Having left the tram and traced Menlove Gardens West, North, and South, he realized there was no such road as Menlove Gardens East. He asked a local constable, but was informed that the man had not heard of Qualtrough or Menlove Gardens East.

'There's no such address,' said the policeman very negatively. 'I'm positive,' he assured the insurance agent.

Wallace was walking away when it suddenly occurred to him that a street directory might be a means of making sure, and he asked the constable if he could direct him to a stationer's before closing time. It was not yet eight o'clock.

Following the constable's directions, Wallace found a newsagent's that was open and because he was afraid of being still later than he already was for the appointment he said something that didn't directly register. He asked, 'Do you know what I'm looking for?' and when the assistant stared at him in a puzzled way he said, 'I'm looking for 25 Menlove Gardens East.' The woman assistant told him there was no such street in Liverpool, and he began hunting through names in alphabetical order to find Qualtrough. But there was no such name in the directory. As he closed the list of names in the directory it occurred to him that he might have been the victim of a hoax, for there were people who had a twisted sense of humour, and would have been amused by his being sent across the city to find an address that didn't exist. He told himself no one would play such a trick on him, and then he remembered his local superintendent, whose name was Crewe. As Crewe lived in a road in an adjacent area he decided to call on him. He reached the house, and rang the bell, but there was no reply. He was out.

So having missed his appointment, he started towards home with mixed feelings, uppermost of which was an acute annoyance. Then he returned to thoughts about his nervous wife and her fear of intruders, and he wondered if she had secured the bolts on the door in her usual way, for she knew that he kept money loose in the house to pay collected premiums until he could bank the money. Upon occasion there was more than fifty pounds in paid premiums.

Had some unknown lured his wife away just to get at the money he had collected?

He became suddenly anxious to get back to Julia for reassurance, only to arrive too late. He found her, lying on a mackintosh on the hearth with her head beaten in and blood drenching her hair.

That was the story the constable he had called listened to. The man was so engrossed in the strange narrative that he made no notes, but rose to his feet and suggested that they search the house together. He had already contacted his sergeant, and the latter arrived with Detective Superintendent Moore when they were going through the house room by room. Then began the endless flow of questions, during which Moore suddenly inquired, 'Didn't you scream or shout?'

Wallace looked at Moore.

'No,' he said. 'I lit the gas. I thought she might be in a fit and I could help her.'

It was about eleven that night when the questions ebbed and

a ruminating Moore suggested to the man who had just lost his wife that he must not think of spending the remainder of the night in the house of death.

'Haven't you got a friend who can put you up?' he asked. 'Or what about your sister-in-law?'

Then began a period when Herbert Wallace lived like a man in a dream. He went through the daily motions of living, and there was a continuous stream of police officers most of whom wanted to ask questions until his head spun. He attended conferences and answered questions—always questions. He saw the same faces in rotation, Superintendent Moore and his fellow superintendent, Thomas, and then Inspector Gold whose face was replaced by officers whose names he did not remember.

He was told that he had to make a statement about what had happened, and it was taken down in longhand and he signed his name. A day or so later Superintendent Thomas gave him a piece of news. The 'phone call to the City Café had been traced to a call box only a quarter of a mile from his own house. It was something the local superintendent appeared to find of particular interest, and he renewed his questions about the 'phone call. Wallace gathered that something bothered the man. Did he think it might have been a hoax after all, as he himself had wondered?

'Possibly,' said Thomas in an enigmatic tone. 'Or a fake, perhaps.'

But he did not clarify his meaning, though he continued to look thoughtful.

In truth Wallace had pondered the mystery of this mysterious address that did not exist from the time he had heard the Johnstons at the back door of their house in Wolverton Street. That had been about a quarter to nine, a few minutes before he saw the wall and furniture splashed with Julia's blood. But he had also pondered a minor mystery which, now he came to think of it a day or two later, seemed significant. One of the kitchen cabinets had been broken open, as the police had found, and a cash-box had been emptied and then placed on the shelf. There had been about four pounds in the empty cash-box. It was the box where he kept insurance premiums, which were made up every Wednesday, when he totted up the total. Then he had found the vase with five pounds in it. 'They didn't take that,' he said to Johnston. Now all these details seemed to add to something he did not understand as he saw Thomas looking at him in that strange manner.

That was when he recalled the words of one of the other policemen when he referred to the mackintosh on which Julia's head lay. It was 'as though,' the man had said, 'the body was a living person and you were trying to make it comfortable.'

Wallace saw Thomas's look, and shivered.

However, the police had made their own examinations and had arrived at a number of inferences that remained secret until some time later. For instance, they had found a clot of blood in the bathroom and had observed that there were no damp towels, while a small blood smear was found on one of the notes in the vase in the back room. But there was an absence of fingerprints and no signs of any force being used to effect entry. The locks on both doors of the house, front and rear, were found to be defective and were not opened easily or readily.

The police surgeon who had been summoned arrived at about ten o'clock, an hour before Herbert Wallace had been advised to leave for the night. He had found that Mrs Wallace had been dead about four hours, which made the time of death about six o'clock, but it could have been up to half an hour or even an hour later. The police had noted that Wallace was a persistent smoker when he was cogitating or perturbed. He was certainly dapper in appearance, with hair parted on the left, gold-framed spectacles, a neat moustache, and a tall stiff white collar with a speckled tie.

'A trim-looking man,' as one police officer described his appearance.

It was the day after the murder that the charwoman who did some occasional work for Julia Wallace told the police there were two objects missing from the house since she had come to work on January 7th. One was a small kitchen poker and the other was a slim iron bar for cleaning under the gas-fire in the living-room.

Was one of these used as a murder weapon? Or even both?

A search of drains and waste ground in the area failed to find them, or, for that matter, any other possible weapons. Wallace had given the police a list of friends and acquaintances his wife could conceivably have admitted into the house, though none of the names seemed likely. This procedure was a to and fro movement that was merely carrying the police back over the former ground they had considered, while Thomas seemed to be digging into his own theory that the mystery of Qualtrough, the man who was never found and never sighted, might have been designed to provide someone with an alibi. Who that someone might be he carefully did not say.

Shortly after the murder Wallace ran into Beattie, and asked about the alleged telephone message given by the mysterious Qualtrough.

'Can you remember the time you received it?' he asked the chess captain.

'Seven or shortly after.'

Wallace asked him if he could place the time more accurately, and after deliberating Beattie shook his head and said, 'I'm afraid I can't.'

But on the day following his meeting with the chess captain there was another summons to call in and see the police, when Superintendent Moore and Inspector Gold confronted Wallace, and from what they said they already knew of the meeting with Beattie and the insurance agent's answer.

'I had been hoping for a more definite time,' said Wallace.

Which meant that so far as the police were concerned the time could not be placed. Further, the outcome of that meeting had not provided any satisfactory answer. Indeed, the whole affair about Qualtrough was unsatisfactory.

Again Wallace left the police station in Liverpool with no feeling of having advanced towards making the overall mystery any clearer. But by now he knew he must be under suspicion by the police, and there were some fairly broad hints in the Press about possible new developments. Indeed, it is reasonable to believe that by this time Wallace had become confused as to what he had said and what he had only imagined he had, but all the statements made by him during this time were dutifully signed by the officers questioning him and working to get some enlargement of the facts.

The police found that he began contradicting some of the things he had said. His confusion grew, but this could have been due to worry about not only the murder but the possible effect it had on his job, although throughout his troubles the Prudential had been most considerate of him and his position, and he had no resultant money worries.

But the case was coming to a climax. This was echoed in the Press and he was cast into a deep personal gloom, when a game of chess afforded no relaxation to his mind or his body. He was sleeping only fitfully and having long broken nights.

Then came the day he was dreading. He was visited again by the police and this time he found himself under arrest.

The day was February 2nd. He was cautioned and formally charged with the wilful murder of Julia Wallace. He blinked rapidly behind his spectacles which gave him an owl-like appearance when he dropped his chin.

'What can I answer to this charge,' he inquired, 'of which I am absolutely innocent?'

His answer took nearly three months, and in that time Liverpool was afforded the sight of a veritable *cause célèbre* that had been enacted on its own doorstep. Indeed, it is not unreasonable to assert that the Wallace case was the city's most memorable murder and trial that can be recalled within living memory. It was certainly the most notorious.

Following the customary proceedings in the magistrates' court the eventual trial opened in St George's Hall, Liverpool, on the 22nd April, when the first spring flowers were in bloom, before

Mr Justice Wright. The court was naturally crowded for the hearing when the clerk of the court spoke in solemn terms as he read aloud the indictment.

'Members of the jury, the prisoner at the bar, William Herbert Wallace,' he intoned, 'is indicted and the charge against him is murder, in that on the twentieth day of January, 1931, at Liverpool, he murdered Julia Wallace. Upon this indictment he has been arraigned, upon his arraignment he has pleaded that he is not guilty and has put himself upon his country, which country you are, and it is for you to inquire whether he be guilty or not guilty and to hearken to the evidence.'

When the proceedings opened the public expected that at last the identity of the unknown telephone caller Qualtrough was about to be revealed. But they were disappointed, for the essential mystery remained, and it has continued to puzzle the people of Liverpool.

The prosecution began with a direct attack.

'The suggestion of the Crown,' the prosecution said, 'is that the person who rang up from that box is the prisoner himself.'

At that a sharp intake of breath could be heard like a cut-off hiss among the public seats. It ended in a ragged sigh of sound. The man in the dock braced his shoulders, for a deadly die had been cast. His life had been placed on the line.

He looked at the jury. They remained watching the prosecuting counsel stroking the wood of the jury box as he would a creature that had to be lulled into complacency.

After a brief interval he went on: 'You may consider that somebody in making that appointment was wanting to get him out of the way the next night, or you may think that he wanted people to believe that someone wanted him out of the way the next night.' He continued, 'You may think that all these conversations with the conductors are natural or unnatural,' and listed a further objection. 'The taking out of the watch, so that the police officer should know exactly what time he was there, you may think of some importance.' Then his mood apparently changed. 'Why on earth should he have felt suspicious,' he inquired, 'because someone had given him the wrong address it is difficult to gather.' Then he began to hurry the arguments, speaking more rapidly and with emphasis.

'Supposing you came to the conclusion that those doors were never shut against him'—he paused—'you then find a man, who could perfectly well get in if he wanted to, pretending that he cannot get in. You might have pictured a cry of agony, bitter sorrow. But what happens? He comes out and says, "Come and see. She has been killed." '

He went on listing further points to objections, and concluded by asking whether the defendant had shown signs of being a broken-hearted husband, 'or whether he remained, apparently, extremely cold and collected since the murder?'

The court was stunned into silence as he added these words: 'If you think that the evidence laid before you leads irresistibly to the conclusion beyond all reasonable doubt that this man, for some reason that we cannot define, killed his wife that night, you will have no hesitation in doing your duty.'

It had been a bleak summation, and it was to become even bleaker and the outlook even blacker for the man in the dock.

There were a host of answers to questions that seemed to him utterly irrelevant, as when a waitress was asked from the witness box if the City Café, in North John Street, was a big place?

'Yes,' she said.

Or if there were many tables?

'Yes,' she said.

Or if a chess club uses those tables on certain days?

'Yes,' she said.

The monotonous repetition of answers to drab questions of unenlivened fact must have wearied both general public and the jury. But the intention was clear. To make the grinding process of the law, like the mills of the gods, exceeding fine as well as exceeding slow. But the prosecution might have quickened up the slow motion if he had not consulted the jury so many times with what they might think was curious. I doubt very much whether they thought so many points were in the least bit curious. But of course it is the way of the law to imagine something to be curious that to ordinary persons might be plain and matter-of-fact.

However, there was, in its turn, a curious contradiction on the part of the prisoner which did not have to be spelled out to the jury. It has been commented on several times in the past.

This was when Wallace, before setting out for Menlove Gardens, whatever the chosen direction of the compass, had said to Julia just before he left to be sure and bolt the door, because there had been a number of break-ins in the past nights. He had said he remembered the occasion clearly. However, there was a different version of what took place. For instance, in the first statement, which had been taken down by the constable without any reference to notes he had said, 'My wife returned and she bolted the back-yard door,' but in a later statement he had claimed, 'She closed the door. I do not remember hearing her bolt it.'

Small wonder the prosecution termed this a very curious contradiction, yet it could in fact have been a curiously simple error, if one wants to beg the description. What was a fact was that he had not bolted the back door, but had remembered later that the back-door bolt had a habit of being difficult to open.

Or was it simply a case of a man overlooking what he thought he had told his wife?

But with the mystery of Menlove Gardens East to hold their attention and interest the court must have seemed anxious to consider the wider implications of the address that never was. So perhaps they were not particularly desirous to have another 'curious' molehill held up and inspected in the hope that it might be considered a mountain.

But there were errors and contradictions in pertinent details as one man revealed. He was Professor MacFall of Liverpool University. He held the chair in Forensic Medicine in that university, and he was an examiner in medical jurisprudence in two

Scots universities, those of Glasgow and Edinburgh, and one English, that of Birmingham. When he was called he delivered testimony about signs of post-mortem rigidity, which he said occurred about two hours after death. He was interrupted by the prosecution counsel who asked him, 'Don't you mean three hours after?'

With no show of being flustered, the professor said, 'Yes, three hours after.'

But this was no comedy of errors, for a life was at stake. In the same way a great deal of explanation and even contradiction was made about the mackintosh on the hearth. First Wallace had told Mrs Johnston it was his, and three policemen corroborated it. But in the witness box Superintendent Moore said in evidence, 'Is this your mackintosh?' The testimony went on as follows: 'He stooped slightly and put his left hand to his chin. I looked at him and he made no reply for probably half a minute or so.' The superintendent paused, as though weighing his choice of words. He continued: 'Then he said, "If there are two patches on the inside it is mine." We found the two patches and he said, "It is mine." '

The defence asked him, 'What inference do you draw from his hesitation when he had already acknowledged it to four different people, three of them policemen?'

Moore replied, 'That he was beginning to think the mackintosh dangerous.'

It seemed that Wallace was beset by dangers.

Even when his own counsel addressed the jury, for he told them, 'It can be proved that this perfectly normal man was behaving perfectly normally throughout January 19th and 20th, which would mean, if he were guilty, that, contemplating this frightful crime, he was going about his daily business and showing no signs of it.'

Perhaps that was not the right note to strike, but there came something more forthright later, when the defence counsel referred to Wallace's demeanour in the witness box. He told the jury that it was that of an absolutely innocent man, but somehow the twelve persons in the jury box did not look impressed, even when the defence went on by addressing them.

'Members of the jury,' he said, making it sound like a challenge, 'are you going to convict that man of murder? Can you conceive such a man doing such a thing as this?'

Then came the prosecution's closing speech, with further suggestions and rhetorical questions, and in court there was renewed shuffling of feet in St George's Hall. But the words were clear enough.

'I am bound to suggest to you, on the part of the Crown, that the evidence connecting this man with the message is strong evidence. That the evidence of what that man did when he came back to the house is strong evidence that he was not acting then as an innocent man.' The shuffling had ceased as he went on. 'Do you believe for one moment that he could not get in at that front door? Do you believe that he could not get in at the back? What are the facts? He first says he cannot get in—but Mr and Mrs Johnston are there and Mr Johnston says he will get a key if necessary—then the door opens!'

And so it went on again over ground that had already been well trampled with argument.

The time came at last for the judge to sum up. In a slow, sonorous voice Mr Justice Wright said, 'This murder, I should imagine, must be almost unexampled in the annals of crime.' He went on to give a fair and impartial summing-up that was reasonably favourable to the defence, although he pointed out that the murder was seemingly motiveless. But regarding the divergent statements in the various testimonies he remarked, referring to Wallace, 'When reference is made to discrepancies in his statements I cannot help thinking it is wonderful how his statements are as lucid and consistent as they have been,' and added, 'It appears to me that it is very striking that they are as accurate as they are, and as consistent as they are.'

But seemingly the jury was not impressed.

They found William Herbert Wallace guilty of murder, and when a sad-looking judge inquired, in the time-honoured phrase, if he had anything to say why judgement of death should not be pronounced upon him, he simply said, 'I am not guilty. I don't want to say anything else.' He led the way down the steps to the cell below.

The defence instituted an appeal on the grounds that the verdict had been against the weight of the evidence, which was unusual in itself. The prisoner appeared in Pentonville, and the appeal was heard on May 18th. The next day Wallace heard the appeal court, in the be-robed and be-wigged person of the Lord Chief Justice, announce, 'The court allows the appeal, and the conviction of the court below is quashed.'

But there was no happy homecoming to 29 Wolverton Street, where he had lived with Julia. The neighbours shunned him and some appeared openly hostile, and although the Prudential had kept his job open for him he felt he had achieved nothing more than futility in the shambles of his life, and this preyed on his mind.

He moved to a bungalow in Cheshire. It was called the Summer House, but there was little summer for him in Meadowville Road, Bromborough, and his health collapsed visibly. Less than twenty-two months after his appeal he was dead, leaving the story of a mystery and perhaps an averted miscarriage of justice for future generations to ponder over.

10

SWEDEN

The Secret of the Flames

Shortly after midnight on a cold November night about a month before Christmas a mysterious fire broke out in the small Swedish community of Tjörnarp. With a strong wind blowing at the time the flames swept over an old mill in their path, and when the local firemen arrived they thought that the entire village might be in danger of being engulfed by the noisy and hungry flames.

The fire seemed to have started in the region of Folke Nilsson's mill, and soon it was apparent that not only had the miller lost his mill, but also his house, which was close by. Although the firemen kept their hoses playing on the mill area, which had been the heart of the conflagration, it was a long time before the anger of the fire abated, and tired and smoke-grimed men felt they could relax their efforts. In the small hours they paused to take stock of the damage. The mill and the miller's house were a charred pile of smoking ruins as their boots squelched through rivulets of water.

They found the miller's charred remains. Most of his pyjamas had been burned away, his body was scorched, and most of his face was unrecognizable as human. He had lived alone in a preferred solitude, frugally and with only a few wants. He had used only a single bedroom, and this was where his remains were found when the fire had been quenched. The only man to make a record of his death was the local constable. When the alarm was raised he had reached the village just ahead of the first firemen.

As he told senior police, he had noticed the fire from a good distance off when he was returning to Steffanstorp, and he had turned his car towards the nearest fire depot and then hurried to see what help he could render.

'But I was unlucky,' he said. 'I was too late to save Folke.'

The wooden mill was quickly consumed, but Hedin had seen someone who he had thought was a stranger near the fire when it was in its earlier stages. The State Police were interested in this stranger. No one else had seen him, but that was probably because the buildings in the village were spaced apart at irregular intervals.

'Have you any idea at all who this person could be?' they inquired next day, November 28th, when Hedin drove over to Tjörnarp. 'We don't believe there's been any crime, it was probably just an accident. We'd like to find out just how Nilsson came to be involved in a fire that became an inferno in such a short time.'

But Tore Hedin could only shake his head and repeat what he had seen. However, within a few hours the police knew that what had occurred was no accident, but murder. The doctor who held a post-mortem was very sure of the fact.

'I'd say he was murdered in his sleep,' said the medical man. He pointed to traces of paraffin that had been found in the dead man's lungs. 'There's no question but this was deliberate arson. I'll have to get in touch with Malmö.'

As a result a murder squad was sent from Malmö to make full inquiries. One of the first persons questioned was Tore Hedin.

'We want anything you can tell us about this stranger you saw near the scene of the fire, Hedin,' the senior in the Malmö squad told the constable.

'There's very little to tell,' said Hedin. 'I noticed the man not long after I had alerted the brigade on the way from Steffanstorp. I suddenly saw him near the fire. He wore a cap, but of course I couldn't see his face, and he was moving. But he was carrying something.'

'What was it?' asked Sten Ugander, chief of the Malmö squad.

'It looked to me like a black briefcase, and I seem to recall that the cap had something on it. Something shiny that made it glitter as he turned away. But I was in such a hurry to help deal with the fire, with the firemen arriving post-haste, that I forgot about it until later. But it seemed to be a shield.'

'A shield on a mariner's cap, would you say?'

'Possibly,' said Hedin with a frown of concentration. 'It had a peak that also shone in the light of the fire.'

The squad under Sten Ugander checked with the State Police and a wide area was searched for a man wearing a peaked cap that had a shiny visor, a man who might have worn the cap in some official capacity.

But more alarming was the motive for the fire and the murder, which was now thought to be theft. For not only was the miller known to have what rumour said was a large sum of money in a locked cash-box, but the stout broken-open metal box was found in the charred remains of his gutted bedroom, and the money was missing, as was Nilsson's heavy gold watch, which he had looked upon as an heirloom.

The Swedish detectives from Malmö tested the smashed cash-box for residual fingerprints, but the fire had ruined any chance of a clue being found on the forced and blistered metal, and they had to fall back on their inquiries. They learned that the miller, besides being a frugal man, had been the treasurer of a sort of farmers' co-operative which paid to him a collection of fees. Upon occasion he had as much as five thousand kronor in his home, awaiting clearing by a bank. That was almost three hundred and fifty pounds. However, on further investigation the police realized the extent of the murderer's theft when one farmer from the district told them he had recently paid Nilsson sums amounting to nearly fifteen hundred kronor.

'How recent?' asked Sten Ugander.

'Yesterday afternoon, as a matter of fact.' The man's eyes narrowed as he seemed to consider his own words. 'No chance of it being cleared by the bank, was there? The banks shut too early.'

The detective looked at the lined face, and asked, 'Did he give you a receipt?'

The farmer looked rueful for some moments.

'He did,' he agreed. 'But it most likely went up in the flames with the money.' He rubbed his mouth thoughtfully. 'If it didn't,' he went on, 'and if the money can be traced, then I can soon prove my words. You see, I paid him with thirteen separate hundred-kronor notes and some smaller ones. Well, it's my regular practice to mark all hundred-kronor notes. Always have and always intend to. Makes checking easy in case of mistakes. One can't be too careful with money, I say.'

The detective looked up.

'Then every one of those hundred-kronor notes Nilsson collected,' he said carefully, 'was marked. That right?'

'Yes. They were marked like this,' said the farmer, and he demonstrated how his special mark was made in each corner, quite inconspicuously, so that it would not be noticed unless one was looking for it. 'So if they were not burned, but had been stolen, I can identify my own notes.'

He was advised to say nothing about his marking of the hundred-kronor notes, and Ugander had a confidential notice circulated to banks, business premises, watch-makers and jewellers, for he was keen to discover if there was a lead on the missing gold watch as well as the notes. He was pretty sure that the money had been stolen with the watch. The broken cash-box had been emptied, Ugander was convinced. But he had to wait more than two weeks for a clue to what he suspected. By then it was the middle of December. He received a 'phone call from a local constable who reported that he had seen one of the marked notes.

'You're sure of the marking?' asked the Swedish detective.

'Yes, sir,' said the constable. 'It was shown to me by a man I know well, who remembers exactly how he came to have it.'

'Good. You'd better contact Constable Tore Hedin. He's been

acting as special liaison man for the local police. He is collecting the paper-work.'

The man accordingly 'phoned Hedin at a village not far from Tjörnarp. However, more than another two weeks went by and the Christmas season passed with the New Year looming ahead, and there had been no further word from the constable who had heard of the marked note. When he had an opportunity he called Hedin.

'Has there been any more about those marked notes, Tore?' he asked. 'I just thought I'd ring and find out. Matter of interest, you know, especially as Ugander said you were handling local details.'

Hedin told the other constable that the Malmö detectives were still following up clues that might bring about the arrest of Nilsson's murderer.

'But it takes time,' he reminded the other, 'and everything these days has to be done in triplicate and filed and then initialled. The work tended to pile up over Christmas.'

'Better you than me, Tore,' laughed the local constable.

He rang off. But then he rang a few minutes later, as though he had had an afterthought.

'There's one thing, Tore, I should tell you,' he said. 'I'm still holding the hundred-kronor note. I thought it would be wanted in evidence or something like that. What am I going to do about it? As you know, Ugander's returned to Malmö.'

Hedin thought about the position.

'I'll tell you what you should do,' he decided. 'Release the note. I've got a record of the number in the local file I was making for Ugander. Anyway, some other notes are likely to turn up, especially as Christmas is past and people will be tight for money. All right?'

'Yes. Thanks, Tore. It gets me out of a spot. My friend was asking how long it would be before the police could let him have his money.'

He rang off again, satisfied that a simple police matter had been straightened out without reference to Malmö. But Tore Hedin was still looking at his file of notes on the Nilsson case. The paper-work was indeed growing, for Ugander and his men were thorough in their documentation and detail of separate items, and this wasn't the first inquiry Hedin had received about the note that had turned up.

Ugander had spoken about it before, and remarked that it was curious that none of the other thirteen hundred-kronor notes had been reported to the police. Each time Hedin had said he supposed it took time for the larger notes to get into circulation. The Swedish detective had agreed, 'I suppose so. Well, keep checking things out.'

But a person who had noticed a change in Hedin was his mother. She and his father were farming folk, the latter elderly and retired. Her son Tore was twenty-five and had joined the Swedish police, but he seemed to be a restless young man who found it hard to settle down with farmers in an agricultural locality. However, his mother had high hopes that the young girl he had become attached to might work a change in him. She thought her son was really in love with the girl, whose name was Ulla Osterbeg. She was a nurse in an old people's home in Hurva, and four years younger than her policeman fiancé. But she suffered from Tore Hedin's frequent outbursts of temper. When around Christmas time she asked him if anything was the matter he told her that he had been living under some strain.

'I get ratty, Ulla,' he assured the girl, 'only because there's unusual pressure on me these days since the Nilsson murder. I have to keep travelling to make sure I have checked on all the work I have to do for the Malmö squad, and it doesn't seem to be getting any lighter.'

There had been talk about bringing forward their wedding in the late spring or summer, but they had reached no agreement and the son's mother waited patiently for a word from the girl she was looking forward to greeting as her daughter-in-law, but with

August more than half over she seemed doomed to disappointment. But then something happened on August 20th, 1952, nine months after the fire that burned out Folke Nilsson's home and mill. That was the day Ulla arrived at the old people's home swathed in bandages.

'Good God, what on earth's happened!' exclaimed Dr Oskar Frenning.

He removed the bandages and stared at the girl's face. It was covered with bruises, as though she had been beaten. She told him tearfully that on the previous evening Tore had arrived at her home and beckoned her to come into her room. With no explanation he had shut the door and at once begun hitting her in the face with his fists. He had knocked out several of her teeth. She had screamed and he had stuffed his handkerchief into her mouth to silence the sound. After that he had handcuffed her with his police regulation 'cuffs, and then continued smacking her face and beating her with his fists.

'He must be mad,' said an outraged Dr Frenning, starting to work on the young nurse's face. 'This may need plastic surgery,' he warned her. 'It's going to take a long while for the marks and bruises to heal. I'd better do something about your mouth, too.'

The doctor was obviously very angry by the treatment to which the girl had been subjected. After doing what he could to make her more comfortable he had told her to go home and rest and take a sedative for her nerves.

'No man should have treated you in this way, Ulla,' he protested. 'I'm going to get in touch with Hedin's superiors. Something has to be done about this.'

The girl protested.

'Please,' she said. 'I don't want trouble.'

'Trouble!' snorted the doctor. 'You've had your share of that.'

As a result of what had happened Sten Ugander was contacted in Malmö, since a man under his authority was concerned. He was both shocked and amazed at what Dr Frenning told him, and promised that Hedin should answer to him for his brutal treatment of the girl who was understood to be about to marry him.

'Though I wouldn't like to say there'll be any wedding after this,' Ugander said bluntly.

He rang through to Hedin's senior in the State Police and told him that Tore Hedin was being suspended immediately, and that there would be an official inquiry into his conduct. The night of August 22nd was close and humid and Ugander could not get to sleep. It was nearly two in the morning when he was wakened by the telephone ringing. The speaker was a police officer who was calling to report that a fire had broken out in the small community of Kvarlov, and he couldn't reach the man who should be on duty.

'What's the constable's name?' asked Ugander.

'Tore Hedin.'

Ugander was suddenly wide awake. The last vestiges of sleep left him like a tossed-aside blanket, and he demanded, 'What about the fire?'

The caller appeared to think about his reply until he said hurriedly, 'It's about Hedin's parents. I have been trying to get hold of Hedin about the fire. I'm afraid the old couple had no chance.'

'What do you mean, man?' snapped Ugander.

'They were burned to death.'

Ugander sat on the side of the bed like a man transfixed. Another question from the man on the 'phone brought back his attention to the present.

'Both of them?'

'Yes, sir. It's a terrible tragedy. Of course, I know that Hedin has been suspended, but I thought that in the circumstances he should be notified of what has happened.'

'Of course,' said Ugander. 'As soon as Hedin is alerted let me know, and ring through if there's any further information at all.'

The Swedish detective cradled the instrument and sat looking at it in puzzlement. He suddenly felt that there was more than the original mystery in what had happened to Hedin's parents. Within a few hours he was reading an account of the fire, which had consumed the home of Hedin's elderly parents. According to the firemen who had been called to the scene of the blaze, the heat had been so intense that they had been forced back.

'It didn't seem like any ordinary fire in a rural area,' said one witness whose words were reported in the Press later. 'I'd say it was more like the fire at Tjörnarp, where that miller who lived on his own was burned to death.'

Ugander read this account with frowning interest, noting especially a reference to Tore Hedin having been seen in the vicinity of his parents' home about nine o'clock on the previous evening. Hedin had been observed getting into his car by someone who recognized him and his car. However, by the time the fire had broken out it was past one in the morning, and according to statements made by the villagers in Kvarlov none of them had seen Tore Hedin for the past four hours.

The Malmö detective chief tried to get through to any police post to which Hedin might have driven in that sparsely populated area of hills and woodlands with tall stands of timber, but all his inquiries and attempts to reach the constable who had been suspended were of no avail and ended in frustration. Indeed, Tore Hedin's continued absence was both inexplicable and mysterious, for by now the constable should have rung through on his own and made contact with a senior policeman. Of course, there could have been an accident, a car crash, for instance, and if it had occurred somewhere in the hills there was no telling how long such a delay could extend.

Meantime he had not been told of the loss of his parents, something that worried Ugander as a conscientious detective chief.

But it was another conflagration that informed the Malmö chief that again disaster had struck. This time at the old people's home near Hurva. As soon as the report came through from an alarmed official, Ugander dressed in a hurry, got in touch with his police driver, and was driven at speed to the village of Hurva, which lay in a fold of the hills shrouded in darkness. But this night the village where Ulla Osterbeg was a nurse was well illuminated. From several miles away the police driver and his passenger watched the wavering light grow larger, until they swept round a bend and saw the devastation of smouldering timbers that told a grim tale.

The detective chief was very soon busy with the task of answering firemen's questions and hearing what the staff could tell him of the outbreak. Rescuers had managed to save the dozen or so inmates, who crouched huddled together under some blankets looking benumbed and shocked as they stared at the now dying patches of flame. The oldest of the rescued patients was said to be over a hundred. But the bodies of the victims who had succumbed to the holocaust had been moved away, out of sight.

Dr Frenning came over and spoke to the detective.

'A terrible thing to have happened so suddenly,' he mourned. 'In the middle of the night as it seemed, without warning. And poor Ulla—her body is over there, near the gutted office of the matron of the home. The remains are not a pleasant sight, and I speak as a medical man, Ugander.'

'I'd like to take a look at the body, doctor,' the detective said, as though some thought had suddenly come to him.

'Well, come this way,' said Dr Frenning, giving the other a quizzical look.

It did not take the man who had spent his career in the investigation of crime many minutes to decide that poor Ulla Osterbeg had been the victim of murder. Several of the victims had had their heads smashed by a killer who had gone berserk. One of the victims was the matron of the home, Agnes Lunden. In the room where she lay there was fresh blood beside a blood-stained axe. But there was a further mystery.

She was not lying on her own bed. She was lying on the fire-wrecked bed of Ulla Osterbeg.

Close examination proved that both women had been murdered

in their beds, seemingly before the fire broke out, or was deliberately started. That was now to be considered as a possibility. Why had the two women changed beds?

While Malmö arson experts were considering the implication of the grim find at the old people's home Ugander sent out an urgent message.

'Arrest Tore Hedin!'

Throughout all neighbouring districts police converged in a drive to find the wanted constable who had been suspended.

'He's got to be found,' ordered Sten Ugander, 'before his crazed lust results in more victims being found with their heads beaten in.'

Fresh radio descriptions were broadcast and photographs of the wanted Hedin were circulated throughout Sweden, and to police authorities elsewhere in the capitals and large cities of Scandinavia. For a time the man-hunt took precedence over other crimes while the work of the arson experts went ahead with making a meticulous examination both in Hurva and Kvarlov.

It was found that neither the elderly retired farmer Per Hedin, nor his somewhat younger wife, Hilda, had died from the fury of the flames. They had been slaughtered in their beds. Their heads had been smashed in with some heavy and sharp weapon, such as an axe or a hatchet. But what struck a reminiscent note with Ugander was the finding of traces of paraffin over the bodies. They had not only been murdered, like the first victim of this grisly series of violent crimes, Folke Nilsson the miller, but their bodies had been deliberately set alight to start a fire.

The growing sense of outrage at the crimes made the police redouble their efforts. Most of them worked longer shifts in order to apprehend the man who was now believed to have gone crazy. Special guards were mounted in homes and villages where he might be lurking in order to renew his maniacal attacks, and patrols covered outlying districts and a network of regular reports was instituted.

It was a member of the State Police who found the missing

Hedin's car. They had been searching the shores of Lake Bosarpasjon, some fifty miles to the north-east of Hurva. They had cleared away some undergrowth and thorny thickets when one of the men saw a gleam of colour between a screen of small leaves. It came from the cellulose of a concealed car.

The thickets were cleared and the familiar sight of Hedin's vehicle was discovered. Two objects had been left on the vinyl of the back seat. One was the removed silver shield of Hedin's uniform cap, which had been tossed aside. The second was a black briefcase. Both had already featured at length in the murder of the miller and the fire that had burned his body.

Inside the briefcase the State Police found a lengthy report by a man whose mind had become mentally deranged. It was written in the style familiar to a man making a statement to his superiors. He described himself with the title of 'Murderer', and gave his address as 'Unknown'. The words were addressed in the first person, and read:

'The telephone rings, the police run around searching for me. But you have not found me. My abandoned car you have found, which is something. If you want to solve a riddle search the water, should you think that I am there. Yes, I will now tell what I have done, and why, so you will not have to lie to the curious public.

'Well, sirs, in September 1943 I set Gustavshill's on fire. And the reason was that I had stolen oats out of the loft to feed my horse at home, because my father starved him. And to hide that I put a match to the straw before I left. Then in the autumn of 1946 I stole the motorbike number L150 in Kristianstad and abandoned it in Asum. In November 1951—to be exact at two-thirty a.m. on the 28th—I killed Folke Nilsson in Tjörnarp, and at three a.m. on the very same day I set his property on fire. The reason was need of money, and I got hold of 4360 kronor on the said occasion.

'Now the reason is that I have been deceived by the girl who has meant so much to me. She has acted towards me in a treacherous way, and for that I pay like this. The 21st of August at midnight I killed my mother and father and set fire to their house. After that I drove to the deceitful girl in Hurva and arrived there at twelve-forty a.m. After studying the most suitable way to do it, I killed her and the matron at one-thirty a.m., and then, at about two a.m., I set the nursing home on fire, after having soaked it well with paraffin.

'Well, I am finishing now, and I hope that you can interpret it as suits you best. In the hope that only facts will be given to the Press, I finish. I regret that I did not become a detective. If I had many unsolved crimes would have been cleared up, because that is—shall I be honest with you?—the only thing for which I would be of any good.

'It is four a.m. on August 22nd, 1952, and now I finish this and my deplorable life and hope that I will be understood and forgiven by those who have the ability and the desire to do so.

'Merry, quiet, and sensible, I go to my death now that everything is fulfilled.

'Signed,

'Tore Hedin
'Murderer
'Address: Unknown.'

There was also a brief postcript, which read: 'P.S. My parents I killed in order that they should not have to see and suffer for what I have done.'

This incredibly self-revealing letter was sent hurriedly to Malmö where it was delivered to Sten Ugander; he was appalled at the contents. It was now obvious that Hedin had been a sick man who had needed the help of a trained psychiatrist. It was help that none of his colleagues in the force had for a moment suspected that he needed. The man's list of crimes and his closing confession had in no sense been good for the soul of a man enduring mental torment, indeed, on the brink of insanity.

The Swedish detective chief drove without delay to the stretch of wild shore where Hedin's car had been uncovered and left under police guard. After a conference it was agreed that the main objective must be to find Hedin. After all, he could have been bluffing to try to draw off pursuit, but somehow Ugander didn't think this was the case. There was stark and naked reality in the words of the confession, rather like the unfleshed bones of a bared skeleton.

'We'll get the Army in,' Ugander decided, 'and cover the lake metre by metre. My hunch is that Hedin wasn't bluffing. He was a man who'd reached the end of his tether, mental and physical.'

Because Hedin had left such a detailed account of his crime, suggesting they 'search the waters', an immediate coverage of the lake was undertaken by a combined party of soldiers and State Police. In due course the bloated and swollen body of Tore Hedin was found little more than fifty yards from the shore. It was submerged between two stone blocks. When he had decided to destroy himself the unhappy man had seemingly waded out into the lake and jumped with the blocks roped to his body.

His watch had stopped at a few minutes after four o'clock.

There remained one outstanding piece of the exposed enigma of Tore Hedin. Together with other Swedish police officers Sten Ugander went over the various clues in an effort to tidy up a case that still had to be confined to official records. When he came to consider the mystery of the moved bodies on the night of the fire at the old people's home, Ugander came to the conclusion that the changed positions had been contrived to baffle an angry Hedin should he have arrived at night to create trouble and another ugly scene. Agnes Lunden, the matron, must have offered to exchange beds with the bandaged Ulla Osterbeg and then retired to the nurse's room. It was believed that in this way she had sought to hold Hedin at bay and reason with him should he arrive in a temper. But the simple subterfuge had been wasted, for Hedin had gone on a murder rampage, and then started the fire in a futile effort to cover his brutal handiwork.

However, one mystery remained, which neither Sten Ugander nor his men solved. It comprised the riddle of what had become of the other hundred-kronor notes that had disappeared from the miller's broken cash-box. Only one of the thirteen marked hundred-kronor notes had been found. None of the other marked notes was ever recovered. Had they been burned by a frightened man scared of his own guilt? It was at least possible.

11

AMERICA

They Called Him the Fox

The mystery started ten days before Christmas in 1927 when little Marion Parker, the twelve-year-old daughter of a Los Angeles banker, Perry M. Parker, was playing with her companions and school-friends. The children were at play in the grounds of Mount Vernon High School when suddenly a stranger appeared in front of Marion. He was a good-looking young man with dark hair of vigorous growth. He smiled at the child and addressed her in a soft-spoken, rather modulated voice.

'Hallo, Marion,' he said, taking her hand. 'I'm afraid I've got some bad news for you.'

The girl looked at him, suddenly scared. She attempted to withdraw her hand, but the young man held on to it.

'Your father's had an accident,' the young man went on, 'and I've come to take you home. I'll explain to Miss Britten. Come along.'

Neona Britten was Marion's teacher. She listened to the young stranger's explanation, and a short while later, buttoned up in her coat and wearing her hat, Marion was seen leaving the school with the stranger. The two turned a corner. From that moment the child holding a stranger's hand was not seen alive again.

The mystery that followed Marion's leaving with the dark-haired young man opened when the child did not return home from the high school. Mrs Parker rang Miss Britten to inquire if there was any reason why Marion had been detained. She was told that her daughter had left earlier than usual, in the company of a stranger.

'As soon as we heard about your husband's accident, Mrs Parker,' said the teacher.

The mother's reaction was immediate.

'Accident! What accident is that?' asked Mrs Parker, with growing alarm in her voice. 'I've heard nothing about one. There must be some mistake.'

'There must be,' said the teacher. 'Perhaps Mr Parker could explain why the young man called and left with Marion.'

But when she rang her husband he was totally mystified about the alleged accident and the young man who had escorted Marion away from school. He got in touch with the police and before long detectives of the Los Angeles force were making inquiries about the well-spoken young man who had led the banker's daughter away with him.

The parents spent a worried night waiting for some news of Marion. The morning post came. It brought a letter in an unfamiliar hand. The writer announced abruptly that their daughter had been kidnapped and would be held to ransom for about fifteen hundred dollars. This was to be paid to Marion's kidnapper. If the money was not paid the child would be put to death.

This brief cold-blooded statement brought Mrs Parker to the verge of collapse.

'Who is this man who has threatened our little girl?' she kept asking the police officers who were grouped around her bed.

The unhappy police could afford her no answer. She clutched Marion's twin sister Marjorie, holding the child to her as though she would never let her go. Some time later, after her husband had induced her to release a tearful Marjorie, the police called again. They asked Perry Parker a number of what they called background questions which would help them to find Marion.

'It's a matter of being patient, Mr Parker,' they told the harassed father. 'You've read the kidnapper's instructions on how the money is to be delivered, and he was careful to put nothing down that could leave a clue for us.'

'So what do you propose?'

'We wait. He'll contact you. He must.'

Perry Parker stared at the police. 'So long as the waiting doesn't take too long. I'm thinking of my wife. This isn't good for her.' He seemed to brace himself. 'She can't take much more of the suspense.'

The way he spoke he seemed to include himself.

However, the police were right. The kidnapper called.

'This is the Fox,' he said in a low voice.

'The Fox' was the name written on the kidnap note, which the police had copied and were studying closely in case the choice of words revealed something about the kidnapper's identity. One thing they were anxious not to reveal to the anxious bank manager was their considered opinion that the threat to Marion's life was merely a bluff. In the second decade of the present century kidnaps and ransom notes were relatively few and far between. Five years had yet to pass before the Lindbergh baby was kidnapped and a special law against kidnappers was passed in a great hurry.

But five years can be a long time to wait for justice. For the Parkers it seemed for ever.

However, eventually the 'phone rang and the soft voice said he was the Fox, calling about Marion; he told the father where he was to take the money, and at what time.

'Marion is well and quite all right,' said the soft-voiced speaker. 'I will bring her with me so that she can return home with you.'

The police had told Parker not to release the kidnap place to any reporters.

'Don't make a note of any time or place given,' they had advised. 'Leave it to us. There are people who like playing hoaxes with us. So in your own interest tell the Press nothing at this stage. Leave it to us,' they repeated.

At the time given by the kidnapper Parker went to the agreed rendezvous where the exchange was to take place and waited for the soft-spoken man to appear with Marion. The police had naturally been alerted, and detectives waited under cover for the Fox to show himself. But the Fox had chosen a good name for himself; he certainly had the instincts of that animal, as well as its cunning. For two hours Perry Parker waited with a parcel of ransom money, while, keeping well screened, the detectives waited to spring out on the man who had abducted Marion Parker.

But after a couple of hours had passed the police knew that something had gone wrong with the plan. The Fox was not intending to show himself. It is possible that in some way he had become alerted to the trap that had been set for him, and was not going to spring it although the police had made sure they had kept well away from the rendezvous.

So a very disappointed father was not reunited with his daughter, and he finally walked away disconsolately from the place where he was to meet her.

When he returned to his family and reported failure his wife broke down again. She was put to bed by a husband who had no relish for his evening meal, and who spent a long wakeful night contemplating the approach of what was to be a sad Christmas for the small family.

When he fell asleep the long night was almost over. The next morning he almost ran to the post to find a fresh letter from the Fox awaited him. There was a grim and ominous note to the words he read.

The Fox wrote:

'When I asked you over the 'phone to give me your word of honour as a Christian and an honest businessman not to try a trap or tip the police you did not answer. Two closed cars followed yours, and you know why. I am ashamed of you. You lied and schemed to come my way and grab me and the girl too. Your daughter saw you and watched your work. Then she drove away broken-hearted because you could not have her in spite of my willingness. You are insane to ignore my terms and tamper with your daughter's death. When I call I will tell you where to go and how to go. So if you go, don't have your friends following. Pray to God for forgiveness for your mistake last night. If you want aid against me, ask God, not man. The Fox.'

When Parker unfolded this letter two brief notes had fallen from its folds. Both were written in a hand he easily recognized as Marion's school-girlish characters. One was couched in a tone of pleading. It said:

'Dear Daddy and Mother—Daddy, please don't bring anyone with you today. I am sorry for what happened last night. We drove right by the house and I cried all the time. If you don't meet us this morning you will never see me again. Love to all, Marion.'

The words brought tears to the banker's eyes. It was a while before he could blink them away to read the shorter note. When he did the tears gushed out again from the eyes of the stricken father, for his daughter had written three sentences that left him numbed. Her note said:

'Please, Daddy, I want to come home this morning. This is your last chance. Be sure and come by yourself or you won't see me again.'

As soon as the police read the letter and the two notes it was plain that the child had written these latter under compulsion for fear of what would happen to her if her father did not obey the Fox's instructions. The words were meant to instil fear of the dread consequences of disobeying someone who was either crazy or enjoyed tormenting a child with what amounted to sadistic intent. She had been terrorized by the sinister alternative to rejection of the demand in the ransom note, and this time the police decided to keep well away from any rendezvous that might be suggested by the Fox when he rang, as they knew he would.

The soft-spoken voice, not much above a whisper of sound, called again, announcing that he was the Fox. Perry Parker felt the telephone glued to his ear as he listened to the quiet words, words he would never forget. Nor would wish to remember.

Speaking of their exchange of words, and what passed between him and the Fox, he later gave the appalled detectives a grim account of what ensued. Referring to the unknown and mysterious Fox, he said:

'He told me to meet him at Manhattan Place and park my car in the place where many other cars are parked, and turn off my lights. I said to him, "For God's sake will you have my little girl?" He said he would. I told him I had the assurance of the police that he would not be covered, that I wanted my little girl back and would bring the money. The Fox answered, "All right. Leave in five minutes." I drove to the place and turned off my lights. A fellow drove by once in a small open car with a handkerchief over his face, apparently looking things over. Finally he pulled alongside me. He levelled a gun at me and said, "You know what I'm here for? No monkey business. Hand over the money." I said, "Can I see my little girl?" He pulled her up from the other side and showed me her head. He said she was asleep. I thought she was chloroformed. I paid him the money and said, "Can I have her?" He said, "Yes, I'll drive down a little and leave her just down the street." He drove a couple of hundred feet, placed her on the parkway by the kerb and hurried away.'

For a moment he stood unable to speak. He was overcome with emotion that left a tight choking sensation in his throat. He drove his car forward, braked, and ran to his daughter lying on the greensward. But then a terrible anguish swept over him. He stood like a man carved in stone, bending over the shape of his daughter as a searing suspicion pierced his mind. By the road was a little girl who would never smile at her father again.

Marion Parker was dead.

He opened the neck of the winter coat and saw the dried blood. By this time it was dark, and he realized that the bundle of clothes covering Marion was oddly shaped. Then the stark truth sunk deep into his consciousness. The body of his daughter had been mutilated by a fiend. There were neither legs nor arms.

When the news of what had happened in the night of a December's closing day was broadcast, a shock-wave of revulsion swept the whole of California and other states in the West. In the gathering dark Perry Parker had not been able to see his daughter's face. What remained was a horrible caricature of reality. She had been strangled and the ends of the throttling wire drawn up so that her eyelids were kept open. The legs had been savagely hacked from the small body, as well as the arms and her hands below the elbows.

An immediate police search resulted in the finding of the butchered limbs in a park. Most likely they had been hurled into the deserted space by a murderer who then went on to meet the father.

The discovery and the bestiality of the butchery resulted in one of the most intense manhunts ever undertaken by the Los Angeles police, who in their time have dealt with such crimes as the notorious Black Dahlia murders and the Bugsy Siegel underworld shooting. But the killing and butchering of a little girl from a local high school made possibly the grimmest impression on dedicated detectives who worked round the clock in their efforts to find the identity of the brutal criminal who hid himself under the sobriquet of the Fox.

The manhunt they mounted became state-wide when a reward of a hundred thousand dollars was offered for his apprehension, and later nation-wide when eight thousand detectives were eventually taking part in the operation. It has been claimed that at one time there were as many amateur sleuths hunting the Fox as professional. More than a score of suspects were arrested, questioned repeatedly, and at last released when all the clues gave out. One suspect was a woman, and there was a man who actually confessed to the crime. But like the other suspects they were proved not to have been the Fox.

Meantime the closest scrutiny of the murder letters was undertaken in California and elsewhere, in the hope of picking up a fresh clue. For instance, it was asserted that the Fox must have been a man of some culture, speaking quietly and even gently. In the letters he had employed both mathematical symbols and Greek characters. At the top of one of them was the word 'Death' in

Greek letters, bespeaking a flamboyant personality. The letter with this characteristic embellishment was found in a Hollywood fire-alarm box after the remains of Marion had been recovered.

This was an incredible gesture, howbeit an empty one. For the note left in the fire-alarm box threatened the murdered girl's sister. It ran:

'For the trouble you have caused us Marjorie Parker will be the next victim. Nothing can stop the Fox and those who try will know the penalty. If you warn anyone of this second success it will mean your neck.'

The police were convinced by handwriting experts that the writing was the Fox's, but the receipt of the note plunged the Parker family into renewed terror. Their police protection was trebled. At the same time a further examination of the bushes in Elysian Park, where Marion's remains had been found, was undertaken. For after dismembering the child's body the Fox had rolled up the remains in rags, including a shirt and a towel. Laundered and ironed, these relics provided a new clue, the first which led eventually to the identification of Los Angeles's most-wanted murderer.

It was a laundry mark made on the cleansed towel. Detectives traced it to an apartment house where a young man named Evans lodged. They found him asleep in bed, and when he heard the reason for his being disturbed he sprang out of his bedclothes and dressed, seemingly very anxious to help the police in any way he could.

So convincing was the act by Evans that the police left to report back to a superior. It was the senior officer who became immediately suspicious of Evan's identity. He rushed his squad back to the apartment house, but by then the Fox had fled, and although the Los Angeles police searched for him it was clear that he had escaped. The detectives found bloodstains in the apartment of the helpful Evans, who had bluffed the police with his false geniality and *bonhomie*. These stains were in the bathroom. They also found a reverse signature on a blotting-pad. When reversed they saw Marion's childish characters a trifle smudged. The most pertinent clue was on a shirt which had been wrapped round part of the girl's torso. The same initials were on Evans's shirt.

But in his flight the Fox had not been cunning enough. He had overlooked something. This was no less than a photograph of himself. It had become wedged in the back of a drawer in a chest.

Copies of the photo were distributed to reporters and publicity agents as well as the police. Within a few hours the photo was identified as that of William Edward Hickman. Barely a year before he had graduated with honours from another high school, one in Kansas City. He had lived a family life with his widowed mother and his brother and sister.

Now the handwriting experts were proved right. The Fox's letters had been penned by a man with claims to being cultured. Hickman had been a good scholar in languages, modern and classical. By this time the story of the young man identified as the brutal and unfeeling Fox was being told throughout the United States. He had become a bank clerk following his graduation, and then, as curious chance would have it, he had secured a post in a bank in Los Angeles—the same bank where Perry Parker was a senior bank official. Because Marion had occasionally called to visit her father Hickman had become familiar with seeing her when she came to the bank.

But the young man of potential talent had betrayed a criminal leaning. It was said that he had been detected in a number of small forgeries which had brought him to the attention of the police. Family friends had pleaded with the police to be lenient with his youth, but because a bank was somewhere where only persons of trust were employed Hickman went to jail. He went 'inside' firmly convinced that his downfall had been brought about by Marion's father. To him Perry Parker was responsible for his going to prison.

He brooded over what had happened and gradually came to feel hatred for the man responsible for bringing about his conviction. The time came when he was released on parole, but instead of deciding to mend unfortunate and erring ways he lived only to secure what he looked upon as revenge. The young criminal was unable to mend his ways, and probably had little stomach for trying to do so. He stole a car and armed himself with a revolver, possibly encouraged by the examples of the gangsters of that day, the late twenties, when Al Capone flourished and waxed bold and deadly with his murderous henchmen.

Hickman rented an apartment where he plotted in secret how to wreak his revenge on Perry Parker. No one knows what was in his mind at this stage. But possibly a darker mood settled over his spirit the more he brooded over what had happened to him. He thought of kidnapping the daughter of Perry Parker and making him pay. He certainly thought of a ransom for the child's kidnapping, but when murder entered his mind or of what terrible form it would take no one could be sure, for it seemed that Hickman's own mind had been affected by his hate. It had certainly become an obsession.

However, the Los Angeles police had a theory that Hickman and his hatred for Perry Parker climaxed in the child's destruction. Destruction became butchery. Some of them believed that his own suicide would result and he would destroy himself as he had little Marion, for his thinking beyond the kidnap letters was never clear. Was the kidnapping only a means to isolate the man he hated? For the ransom certainly had been a modest sum, and might have been a pretence only, and then he was committed when lust for killing became rampant in a sick mind.

The pursuit of the killer on the run continued for a week, but it ended suddenly on December 22nd, three days before Christmas. At the time the chase of the wanted man came to an end there were leads extending throughout California and into the States of Oregon and Washington. After he had broken from the apartment where he was known as Evans he became completely reckless. He left a trail of marked twenty-dollar bills in a wavering line across the countryside. The money was the ransom Perry Parker had paid. State troopers were on the lookout for the money.

They approached a parked green car, but when their own car slowed the driver of the green car hurriedly made off. The police decided to stop him and make inquiries. This was in Pendleton, Oregon. However, the green car's driver suddenly swerved, circled, and then evaded them on a side-road.

'That's Hickman!' one of them exclaimed. 'That's why he ducked us.'

They gave chase and after pursuit of several miles caught up with the man in the green car when they crowded him over and ordered him to stop. He pulled over and braked as the State troopers produced guns.

'All right. Get your hands up, Hickman,' one ordered. 'This is the end of the line.'

The wanted man started to climb out of the car he had stolen. Then he attempted to make a break for it. He dived towards the door of the car, but the sawn-off shotgun he held between his legs got snagged in his trousers and he fumbled getting it clear and as he opened his legs it fell with a clatter to the ground.

He was given no chance to recover. The State troopers grabbed him and he was under arrest. One of the most wanted men in the US had been captured. When the troopers frisked him they came upon the rest of the twenty-dollar bills. All bore the identifying sign of the notes the police in Los Angeles had secretly marked.

As news of the Fox's capture spread a crowd quickly collected when he was taken to the Pendleton jail, and the police had to cordon off an area to prevent losing their prisoner to a lynch mob, which demonstrated noisily against Hickman and several tried to reach him with their hands.

'Let's have the bastard. We know what to do with him,' they shouted.

The police had to rush reinforcements to the Oregon town, but the men and women making the demonstration against the butcher of Marion Parker continued the calling out and catcalls for hours. The fervour of their vociferous protests and the bitterness of their loathing reached a peak of hysteria at one time when yet additional police had to be summoned. In Pendleton the booing and shouted threats went on all night.

The small town where Hickman had been overhauled by the State troopers was called Echo. The townsfolk of that town had been the first to realize what the stopping of the police car signified, and word of Hickman's arrest spread like a forest fire. They formed a cavalcade which became an escort of cars when Pendleton and the safety of its jail was reached.

In due course, when the excitement had died down somewhat, a cowering Hickman, close to collapse after the noisy demonstrations against him, appeared for questioning about the crime, which was front-page news throughout America, and a veritable Christmas bonus to the Press. He appeared anxious when informed that he would have to be returned to California, but after some minutes he affected an air of bravado, aware that he was able to play to the crowd, especially to the out-of-town reporters.

'I'd have shot you in another minute and made my getaway,' he snarled at them.

This produced some hissing, at which he smiled, though the expression around his face was more a look of strain. There was something plainly on his mind. What this something was became clear when he suddenly demanded, 'Do they hang you or electrocute you in California?'

Someone in the concourse informed him that hanging was the punishment for a capital crime in California. He suddenly looked relieved, as though a mental weight had been removed from his mind.

'That's better,' he said. He even managed another strained smile.

However, when it came to answering point-blank questions about the murder he seemed to recover more than just his equanimity. He even had considerable bounce in his manner, as though he had adjusted to his own resilience. He made light of any suggestion that he had murdered the school-girl because he desired revenge on her father.

'I planned the kidnapping to raise enough money to attend college,' he stated. 'I did not kill her and I wasn't cruel to her. In fact, I really liked her.'

'If you didn't kill her, who did?' retorted an officer who was questioning him.

Hickman hedged and moistened his lips.

'I admit the kidnapping,' he nodded, 'but I didn't do the murder or the cutting up. I was making my living by hold-ups, and thought if I could get someone to work with me there would be less risk. I wanted to get enough money to go to school and pay for my tuition. I reckoned if I could get a thousand dollars I could start next September, and then, no matter how I got it, I would go straight from then on.'

It didn't sound convincing as he continued, 'And then I met a man named Andrew Cramer, who was living an evil life. He was a drug trafficker and had a woman confederate named June Dunning. He asked me what I thought about kidnapping someone, and I thought I would not mind doing it. I happened to remember Mr Parker had a daughter.'

It was less convincing when he related how he had taken Marion to his apartment after leaving the high school, and then he told her that her father had not had an accident. When Hickman sent him some money she would be sent home. It all sounded very glib.

'I told her if she was not good I would have to tie her nose and mouth so that she could not make a noise, and she said, "Please don't. I will promise not to make a noise." So I didn't tie her, and we drove round all that afternoon and went to a show that night. Even went to a picture show, the Rialto. I really didn't intend to do her any harm, and there's where this other man came into it.'

He went on to say that Cramer had taken the girl away, but had not left his address. Because the police had been on the *qui vive* he had sent the ransom notes and had threatened Marion in them. But the next day Cramer had arrived with a suitcase.

'I let out a yell of surprise,' said the man who had become the Fox.

'What did he have in the case?' he was asked.

He hesitated.

'He had just . . .' He started again. 'She was cut right across the middle of the body and her arms—he had fixed them up and he had her dress on her and a little sweater thrown on her face. Of course she was dead,' he added naïvely.

It didn't take the California police long to trace Andrew Cramer to the prison where he had been in jail since the previous July, while June Dunning was proved to be elsewhere at the time of the crime in December.

Hickman was then seen to be a murderer who had murdered alone, though he still clung to an almost incredible belief that Marion was alive even after he had threatened her twin sister Marjorie. 'I've got a message for you from Marion,' he claimed with futile intent on several occasions. But the subterfuge had worn thin with the pretence, and after a number of delays he was at last brought face to face with a judge on February 9th, 1928, fifty-six days after the murder. He stood trial in the Supreme Court of Los Angeles, where the district attorney, the popular Asa J. Keyes, made a dramatic and impassioned argument that the court should 'hang the foul criminal, the perpetrator of the most brutal crime in all history'.

When the trial was in its closing stages, he scoffed at possible insanity as a plea, and then paid tribute to the defence counsel, Attorney Jerome Walsh.

'He has made an admirable fight,' he said almost grudgingly, 'for one who did not deserve it.'

When the jury came to retire they were out only a few minutes longer than half an hour, and they found that Hickman was sane when he committed his murder. Later the judge passed sentence of death, and later still Hickman found he could bring himself to jest about it.

'The State win by a neck,' he declared to reporters, and added almost nonchalantly, 'I still don't know why I killed Marion, but I did, and I'll later take what is coming.'

The University of Chicago made a 'phoned application that he should bequest his body to them for scientific purposes. His rejoinder was included in famous last words, as a senior detective put in wryly.

'I should have my body cut into forty-eight pieces and send a piece to every State in the Union.'

With this sardonic comment William Edward Hickman, dubbed the Fox by thousands who hated him for butchering a little girl, mounted the grim scaffold at San Quentin, the notorious 'Big House' of later generations, and died by hanging, a man who was a mystery and an enigma. To himself as to most who read about his crime.